PRINT
PATTERN
SEW

PRINT PATTERN SEW

BLOCK-PRINTING BASICS
+ SIMPLE SEWING PROJECTS

for an Inspired Wardrobe

JEN HEWETT

PHOTOGRAPHS BY JEN SISKA

ROOST BOOKS
BOULDER
2018

Roost Books
An imprint of Shambhala Publications, Inc.
4720 Walnut Street
Boulder, Colorado 80301
roostbooks.com

9 8 7 6 5 4 3 2 1

First Edition
Printed in China

♾ This edition is printed on acid-free paper that meets
the American National Standards Institute Z39.48
Standard.
♻ Shambhala makes every effort to print on recycled
paper. For more information please visit
www.shambhala.com

Distributed in the United States by Penguin Random
House LLC and in Canada by Random House of Canada
Ltd

Designed by Danielle Deschenes

Library of Congress Cataloging-in-Publication Data
Names: Hewett, Jen, author.
Title: Print, pattern, sew: block-printing basics + simple
sewing projects for an inspired wardrobe / Jen Hewett.
Description: First edition. | Boulder: Roost Books, 2018. |
Includes bibliographical references.
Identifiers: LCCN 2017016294 | ISBN 9781611804621
(hardcover: alk. paper)
Subjects: LCSH: Textile printing. | Repetitive patterns
(Decorative arts) | Dressmaking—Patterns. | Dress
accessories—Patterns.
Classification: LCC TT852 .H49 2017 | DDC 646.4—dc23
LC record available at https://lccn.loc.gov/2017016294

CONTENTS

DEDICATED TO MY FAMILY:

Mom, Dad, Tin, and Gus

INTRODUCTION

Like many people, I developed my own personal style over time. For years, I dressed for the job I had, or to be the person I thought I was supposed to be, or simply to follow the trends that retailers sold me. But now that I'm older and more confident—and have my dream job as an artist—my style reflects who I truly am. I do not take this for granted; it has taken much hard work and experimentation to get to this point in my life and career. Every day as I get dressed, I am grateful that I get to wear clothes that express who I am, what my current mood is, and the work that I plan to do that day.

As a child, clothes were never a big deal to me, mainly because I was required to wear a Catholic school uniform, which was limited to five white blouses, a navy blue sweater, and a plaid skirt. In high school, the uniform became slightly more varied but also much more drab: it consisted of a taupe, pleated wool skirt (for winter) or a khaki A-line polyester skirt (for spring and fall), a brown or cream school sweater, and a brown blazer. The shoes—brown or black penny loafers or oxfords—were sturdy and practical and meant to last the entire school year.

I wore a school uniform for twelve years, yet until I was a teenager I didn't feel my uniform was limiting but, rather, incredibly freeing: I didn't have to think about what I was going to wear each day or worry about standing out even more in my school, where, as one of four African American children, I was an anomaly. Instead, I could focus on the work I had to do that day, which was simply being a student. Putting on that uniform signaled the start of my school day and the moment from which I would try to blend in.

I graduated from Catholic school and attended the University of California at Berkeley, a far less structured environment where I could wear whatever I wanted. (Or wear nothing at all: my first year there, a student made national news for regularly attending classes naked.) For the first time, I started experimenting with my wardrobe. On a daily basis I got to decide who I felt like being at that moment, then choose clothing that would reflect this. Clothes were no longer merely functional items; they had become a way for me to express who I was, and who I wanted to be. At seventeen and away from home for the first time, I started to develop my own style.

My sense of style took a giant leap forward when I later learned printmaking. I took a screenprinting class on a whim, as a creative outlet while working a corporate job, and I was quickly hooked. My initial work was on paper. Then, after a year of selling prints online and at craft fairs, I decided to try screenprinting on fabric, and to sew bags out of the fabric. The bags sold so well that I eventually quit printing on paper altogether and focused on improving my skills as a textile printer.

I was still primarily a screenprinter when, in 2014, I decided to try other forms of printmaking. I embarked on a project I called "52 Weeks of Printmaking," with the goals of experimenting with new print media and creating a print each week. I taught myself how to block print using a soft carving medium instead of linoleum or wood, and I planned to take classes to explore the other forms of printmaking, such as etching, letterpress, and lithography. However, the demands of my day job and of regularly releasing new collections of screenprinted goods meant that I often waited until the very last minute to work on my weekly print. And, since I knew I could quickly execute a compelling block print using a soft block, simple shapes, and complementary colors, I most often ended up creating a block print for my weekly print.

Block printing almost every week like this—I block printed for at least forty-four of the fifty-two weeks— helped me develop my skills, and my prints became more complex. I soon grew to love block printing as much as I loved screenprinting, and the medium had an additional

advantage: unlike screenprinting, with its specialized equipment, block printing is a very accessible craft. It requires only a block, an inexpensive carving tool, and a minimal amount of space.

The same year that I started block printing, I also started to sew my own clothes. By this time, my own style had evolved beyond what was easily available in stores. I was frustrated with the cheap fabrics and shoddy construction of the clothes that were within my budget. (And designers had, at some point, decided to make only miniskirts and maxi skirts, both of which look awkward on my tall frame.) I discovered independent sewing pattern designers, with their modern, unfussy patterns and straightforward, easy-to-understand sewing instructions. I even began to create my own, self-drafted garment patterns. Sewing my own clothing helped me develop a new uniform—one of full skirts and boatnecked blouses, boxy shirts and A-line dresses, all in natural fibers. This time my uniform reflected the working artist I'd become.

Soon my love of block printing and garment sewing merged. By the time I finished "52 Weeks of Printmaking," I was ready to try something more ambitious: to print my own yardage and then sew it into clothing for myself. I had just a few rules for this project: I had to print the fabric by hand (rather than digitally); I had to use either a self-drafted pattern or a pattern from an independent designer; and each garment had to be something I'd actually wear. I called this project "Print, Pattern, Sew," and it became the basis for this book.

"Print, Pattern, Sew" was a breakthrough project for me. My previous printmaking had been on small pieces of fabric for flat applications, such as bags and napkins. For this project, I had to think about how a print would look on a larger scale, as well as on my body. The end result of pushing myself in this new direction is a new wardrobe made up of garments in the colors, cuts, and prints that I prefer. The reward is a wardrobe that is, at its very core, mine.

Through this book I hope to inspire you to create your own hand-printed wardrobe, so you can experience the pleasure of creating—and wearing—truly handmade clothing.

PRINT

PREPARING TO PRINT

Making your own clothes with fabric you've printed yourself is deeply satisfying. In exchange for your time and labor, you receive something that is unique to you, created with your own vision and your own hands. When you make your own clothes, you're not passively subject to whatever trends designers and retailers choose to offer you each season. Rather, making clothes requires both thought and time— the time not only to print and sew but also to deliberate over the fabric, pattern, and fit. Instead of finding something for right now, you contemplate, over time, how to fill a hole in your wardrobe, how to create something that will be worth the effort you will put into it. This does not delay gratification; the reward of a custom garment is partly in the process of making it.

However, enjoying the process does not mean limiting your block-printed projects to garments that take days, rather than hours, to complete. Instead, start with a small, simple project and then work your way toward more complicated projects as you develop your skills. The most important thing, regardless of your skill level, is to create something that reflects your own taste and style.

YOUR BLOCK-PRINTING KIT

BLOCK PRINTING IS ONE OF THE OLDEST FORMS OF PRINTMAKING, so it's no surprise that the tools used to create blocks haven't changed much in thousands of years. The tools are simple—a cutting tool, a block, some ink and a roller to apply it with, and something to print on (in our case, some fabric)—so it's both easy and inexpensive to create your own block-printing kit.

Having the proper tools will help you create crisp, beautiful prints, but even more important than tools is skill. The highest quality, most expensive tools are no substitute for time spent honing your skills. In the same way that I always test my prints on inexpensive muslin first, it is fine to develop your skills using inexpensive tools and materials. Here are the key elements to include in your printing kit.

BLOCK

There are many different types of printing blocks available, and they have varying degrees of hardness. The four most common types of block are wood, linoleum, rubber, and soft synthetic blocks. Wood is the hardest medium, and therefore it is the most difficult to carve. It's great for creating superfine lines and is incredibly durable. Linoleum, which is where the term *linocut* comes from, is softer than wood but is still very durable. Linoleum can also be difficult to carve, but, also like wood, it holds fine lines and details well.

In my own work, I prefer to use either rubber or soft synthetic blocks. These blocks are much softer than wood or linoleum and very easy to carve. Some printmaking purists look down on these types of block because

MIXING AND STORING INK

The screenprinting textile ink comes in a wide variety of colors. You can certainly use an ink straight out of the jar, but I encourage you to mix it with other colors to create your own custom shades.

Always mix way more of a color than you think you'll need: in my experience, you will usually end up needing more, and it's very difficult to remix an exact color match. A good rule of thumb is ¼ cup of ink for each yard of fabric. Always mix your ink in a cup or a jar using a spoon, spatula, or wooden tongue-depressor stick. Mixing ink on an inking plate often leads to having too much ink on the plate, and if there's too much ink on your inking plate, your roller will become gloppy, which means you'll get a muddy print.

There are a number of comprehensive books and classes on color mixing and matching. I am not an expert on the topic, but the process I like to follow is to figure out what the dominant tones of the desired color are, then start with the lighter tone as a base. Want a very light pink? Start with white, then mix in a little bit of red until you get the right shade. If you want a more peachy pink, add in a tiny bit of yellow; for a more lavender pink, add a touch of blue. Keep notes as you go, in case you want to mix more of that color in the future.

Store unused ink in an airtight container away from heat or direct sunlight. It will keep for some time, as long as it's not regularly opened and exposed to air.

they are less durable and tend not to allow as much fine detail as a harder block does. However, soft blocks are very flexible, they work beautifully with the water-based fabric ink I use, and they can easily be cut with a utility knife. All the projects that I have included in this book are meant to be executed using soft, synthetic blocks.

Soft blocks are available in a range of sizes and qualities. I always recommend starting with a block that will take hours—rather than days—to carve, so that you can work through the entire process in just a few sittings. When you're first starting out, I recommend using a block that's no larger than 4 x 6 inches, approximately the size of your hand. Larger blocks require more time to carve as well as more skill to print them evenly.

INK

A number of different inks meant for printing on fabric are available. The two most common are oil-based block-printing ink and water-based textile screenprinting ink. I don't use oil-based block-printing ink because it comes in a limited number of colors, the colors do not mix together well, and it should not be used with soft blocks. (Plus it often has a strong chemical smell.) I prefer to use water-based textile screenprinting ink instead.

Although screenprinting is a very different form of printmaking, its water-based textile inks work very well for block printing on fabric, especially when using soft blocks. They have the additional benefits of being relatively inexpensive and easy to combine to create custom colors. All the projects that I have included in this book are meant to be executed using water-based screen-printing ink intended for textiles.

LINOLEUM-CUTTING TOOL AND BLADES

For the type of block we're using, a lino cutter set, which includes a plastic handle and removable (replaceable) blades of different sizes, will suffice. You'll need to make sure that your blades are sharp, because dull blades carve crumbly lines. Keep replacement blades on hand, and change out your blades as they become dull.

SKETCH PAPER OR SKETCHBOOK

This may seem like an obvious item—every artist and crafter has sketch paper—but it's an important tool. Unless the image you'll be carving is symmetrical on all sides, you will want to sketch out your ideas and final design on paper first, then transfer it onto your block. It's far easier to fix mistakes on paper than to fix them on a block! (Remember that your block will be a mirror image of what actually prints.) I talk a lot more about how to transfer your design from paper onto a block in chapter 2.

LINO CUTTER BLADES

Each blade that comes with your lino cutter set has a different function:

1. **SMALL V**—This blade can carve very fine details. It does not carve very deep lines, however, and it can tear your block if you use too much pressure when you carve. I rarely use this blade, preferring to use the large V blade for fine lines.

2. **LARGE V**—Great for details and outlines, it carves deeper than the small V blade.

3. **SMALL U**—Good for making deep cuts and carving outlines around images with a rounded edge.

4. **SQUARE**—Also good for deep cuts, it works well for carving outlines around images that are made of straight lines.

5. **LARGE U**—Use this to carve large areas. It is also good for beveling the edges of your block.

6. **KNIFE**—Use this to carve very sharp edges. You can also use it to score the outline of your image, creating a trough that will help guide the other blades as you carve and keep them from accidentally nicking your image.

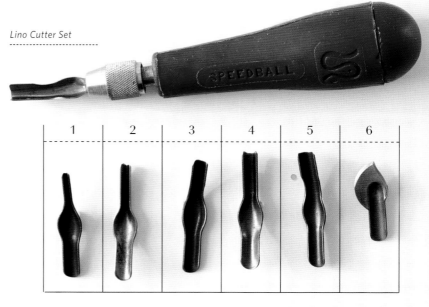

Lino Cutter Set

A. *Sketchbook*

B. *#2 Pencil*

C. *Tracing Paper (for transfer)*

A. *X-acto or Utility Knife*

B. *Baren*

C. *Inking Plate*

D. *Roller*

PENCIL

Another (seemingly) obvious item, the pencil deserves mentioning. Even if you do your sketching with a pen, you will need a regular #2 pencil or softer (and not a mechanical pencil) to transfer your image.

TRACING PAPER

Your carved block will be the mirror image of your design. You'll need tracing paper to transfer this mirror image from your sketch paper to your block. I show you how to do this in chapter 2.

X-ACTO KNIFE OR UTILITY KNIFE

An X-acto knife (also known as a pen knife) is great for neatly trimming away excess bits of your block. If you don't have an X-acto knife or utility knife, you can use scissors or even the knife blade on your lino cutting tool.

BAREN

Originally developed for printing on paper, this is a disc-like tool that helps you apply even pressure to your block to get a sharp print. It's not a necessary tool, but it helps relieve pressure on your hands when you print, so it's nice to have when printing yardage and repeat patterns.

INKING PLATE

You'll need some kind of inking plate to spread out your ink in an even layer before applying it with a roller to your block. Any smooth, flat, and nonporous surface can be used as an inking plate. I use 10 × 10-inch plexiglass squares that I found at a local reuse center. Your local hardware store or plastic supplier may sell inexpensive scraps of plexiglass or acrylic sheets. If you cannot find those items, a flat plate or cookie sheet can work just as well. It is best to have one plate per color so you can experiment with placement, but since you usually only print one color at a time, you can wash the plate between colors if necessary.

BRAYER OR ROLLER

You will use a brayer or roller to spread ink onto your block. Never dip your block directly onto the inking plate; always use a brayer or roller. There are a number of brayer types, the most common of which are the rubber brayer, the foam brayer, and the paint-trim roller.

Although a rubber brayer is the traditional printmaking tool, it's best for use with block-printing inks, rather than the screenprinting ink we'll be using. Because the consistency of screenprinting ink isn't dense enough to adhere to the traditional, hard brayer or foam brayer, I use a paint-trim roller, the smaller type of roller you would use to paint the wood trim in your house. They're available at your hardware store. I prefer roller covers with a low nap, and I always buy a few replacement covers so I can switch colors without waiting until my washed roller cover is dry.

QUILT BATTING

A thin layer of cotton batting (available at most fabric stores) or felt will both protect your printing table and

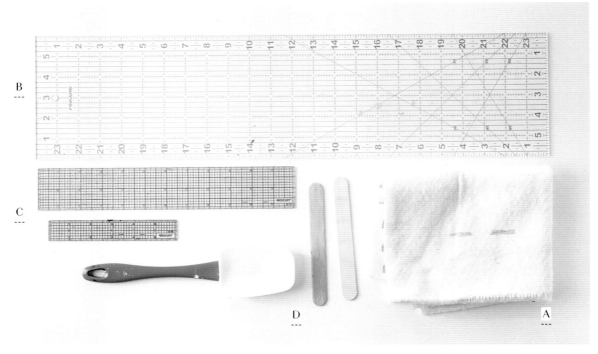

B ---

C ---

D ---

A ---

A. *Quilt Batting*

B. *Quilting Ruler*

C. *Regular Ruler*

D. *Spatula and Wooden Sticks*

provide a soft surface on which to print. Printing on a flat, hard surface with a light padding helps you achieve a more solid print, compensating for any slight irregularities on the surface of your block. The batting should be at least the width of your fabric; I like to use a sheet of batting a couple of feet longer and wider than my printing table.

A. *Tailor's Chalk*

B. *Plastic Containers with Lids*

C. *Muslin*

D. *Notebook*

QUILTING RULER (4 × 24 INCHES OR LONGER)

An indispensable tool, a quilting ruler is a clear, gridded ruler that serves as your guide when creating evenly spaced repeat patterns. I prefer a 36-inch quilting ruler because it is more than half as wide as both of the most common fabric widths, 44 inches and 60 inches.

REGULAR RULER(S)

A large quilting ruler can get unwieldy when measuring small items such as blocks, so I always keep a 6-inch and a 12-inch ruler handy.

SPATULA OR WOODEN STICK

You will need a spatula or wooden stick to scoop inks out of the jar and to mix them. To mix small amounts of ink, I prefer inexpensive wooden tongue-depressor or ice-pop sticks, which are available at craft stores and dollar stores. Keep in mind that wooden sticks are also washable and reusable.

TAILOR'S CHALK

This tool comes in handy for marking your fabric before printing repeat patterns. But use it sparingly: it doesn't always wash out completely.

PLASTIC CONTAINERS WITH LIDS

Store your unused mixed ink in a wide-mouth plastic or glass container. I save yogurt cups and plastic takeout containers for this. I also buy plastic jars from the dollar store when I'm out of used food containers.

MUSLIN

Cotton muslin is an inexpensive and widely available fabric, which makes it great for testing your prints before you start printing on your more expensive garment fabric. I'll talk more about fabric in a moment.

NOTEBOOK OR BINDER

I have a binder where I keep information such as the final measurements for my repeat patterns, the rough formulas I used to develop each custom color, and care information for the different types of base fabrics I buy. I used to write this information on random pieces of paper, but after accidentally throwing away one note too many, I decided to store everything in a binder.

SETTING UP YOUR PRINTING STATION

YOU DON'T NEED A LOT OF SPACE TO MAKE BLOCK PRINTS. In fact, for years I printed yards of fabric on a table pushed against a wall of my old 54-square-foot studio—a room not much larger than a king-sized mattress!

What is essential, whatever size your workspace, is a sturdy table that is a minimum of 28 inches tall. If you're tall like I am, and you plan to print a lot, then you may want a taller table—one that is around waist high will allow you a more comfortable posture while printing. Ideally, your table will be at least as wide as your piece of fabric. However, in my old, tiny studio, I often worked around this by printing half of my fabric's width at a time.

Place your batting or felt on top of your printing table. This layer will protect your table, and, more important, it will create the soft, slightly springy surface essential for block printing. If you find yourself doing a lot of printing, you can create an entire removable printing surface that you place on top of your table. Simply drape a large piece of felt or batting over a wood surface, such as an inexpensive tabletop or flat door from a hardware store or furniture retailer, and staple it to the underside. Store the whole thing in a closet when you're not using it.

Also make sure that you have enough tabletop space for your inking plate, ink, and block. If your table isn't wide enough, any additional, easily accessible flat surface will do (I sometimes use a foldable TV tray table). As you print, you'll find what works for you. Adjust your workstation as you go along.

CHOOSING AND WORKING WITH FABRICS

CHOOSING FABRIC FOR BLOCK PRINTING IS BOTH an aesthetic choice and a practical one. You'll spend a lot of time working with—and eventually wearing—your fabric, so make sure to purchase fabric that appeals to you. On the more practical side, there are a few factors to take into consideration when selecting your fabric.

FIBER TYPE

Fiber refers to a fabric's composition. Fabric can be composed of a natural fiber, such as linen, cotton, silk, or wool, or a synthetic one, such as rayon or polyester. The type of ink we'll be using for the projects in this book does not work on all fibers. My preferred brand of ink, for example, is recommended for use on cotton, linen, rayon, and polyester; check the labels on your jars of ink. I mainly print on linen, cotton, and linen-cotton and cotton-silk blends. These natural fibers can withstand the high temperatures required to heat-set the ink, while synthetics often burn when exposed to an iron that is too hot.

From experience, I've found that fabrics containing cotton or linen both hold a print well and aren't weighed down by the ink. I don't print on pure silk, because the ink does not bind as well to this fabric and also weighs it down, changing the fabric's drape. However, cotton-silk blends print beautifully and are a great alternative for items that require a light-weight fabric with a lot of drape.

DRAPE

Drape refers to how a fabric hangs and flows. Stiff fabrics, such as canvas, tend to have less drape, while more flexible fabrics, such as jersey and voile, have more. Think of the

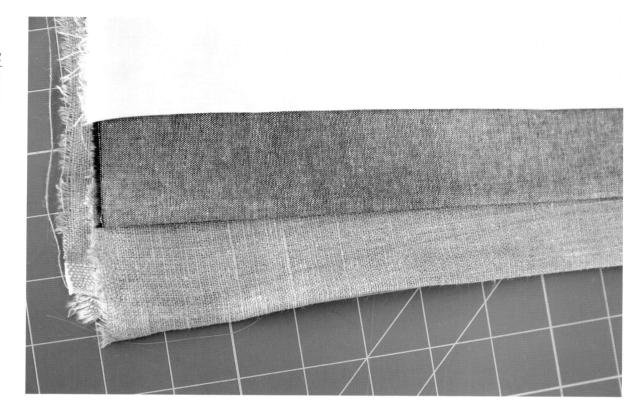

difference between cotton canvas, which is often used for tote bags, and cotton voile, which is used for blouses and scarves. Both are made of the same fiber—cotton—but the canvas is stiff and wouldn't contour to your body, while the voile is fluid and can be easily twisted, for example: canvas does not have much drape, while voile does.

Drape is not an inherently good or bad quality in a fabric. The fabric's end use—that is, whether it will become a tote bag or a blouse—dictates how much drape your choice of fabric should have.

WEIGHT

Distinct from drape, weight has to do with a fabric's thickness, not how it flows. Canvas has both a heavy weight and little drape, but some fabrics are both weighty and drapey, such as crepe, which are often used for suits and dresses. Alternatively, many types of silk and synthetic organzas, which are used in formal dresses, are lightweight fabrics that do not have much drape.

Garments that will get a lot of wear, such as outerwear, or whose seams will be subject to a lot of stress, such as pants and fitted skirts, should usually be made with a heavier, more durable fabric. Blouses and scarves, which do not need to be quite as durable, can be made with lighter-weight fabric.

COLOR

The ink I recommend using for the projects in this book will be fairly translucent when printed. This means that the color of the fabric will show through the ink. This translucence is part of the beauty of block printing, but it also means that you need to take the color of your fabric into consideration when choosing ink colors: a cream-colored fabric may emphasize the yellow undertones of a green or orange ink, for example, while a blue chambray may make white ink appear more gray.

I always recommend printing on light-colored fabrics when you're first starting out. Lighter colors are more forgiving of printing errors, while darker colors often emphasize mistakes. I also personally avoid printing on fabric that has been commercially printed already, or which has a pattern built into its weave (such as a gingham or herringbone), because I find a block print looks too "busy" on top of a fabric's existing pattern.

Buy at least an extra half-yard of the fabric you're planning to use so you can test colors on it. A color is often much darker once it dries, and I've found that a color never looks the same actually printed on the fabric as it did in my head. You don't need to throw out your test fabric, though. You can always line pockets with this fabric, sew it into small bags, or make it into bias tape.

WEAVE AND TEXTURE

A fabric's weave is the way the threads of its warp (which runs the vertical length of the fabric, also called "grain") and the weft (which runs the horizontal width of the fabric, also called "crossgrain") are woven together. The weave impacts the fabric's texture. The easiest type of fabric to print on is one with a plain, dense weave. Fabrics with more complex types of weave, such as twill, herringbone, and jacquard, are more difficult to print on. The texture of these weaves will keep your image from printing evenly.

The printed images or shapes you'll be creating will also determine your fabric choice. In general, fine lines and smaller images print best on smooth, lightweight fabrics, and big blocks of color look better on more textured, heavier fabrics. But those are just general rules: I've printed solid blocks of color on

lightweight fabric to make scarves, for example, and have found the results stunning. Likewise, I printed finer lines on heavy linen for a skirt and loved the effect. The key is to experiment and discover what works for you.

PREPARING YOUR FABRIC FOR PRINTING

ONCE YOU'VE SELECTED YOUR FABRIC, wash it according to the manufacturer's instructions. You should always wash your fabric before printing on it, to preshrink it and to remove any sizing that coats the fabric. (Sizing is a starch-like chemical that is used to coat warp threads during the weaving process.) You want your ink to bind to the fabric; sizing can interfere with this and cause the print to wash out of your fabric even after it's been heat-set. Washing information is usually printed on the end of the cardboard bolt the fabric is wrapped around at the store; be sure to write this information down when you purchase your fabric. I like to cut a small swatch of the fabric and staple it into my notebook, then write the laundering instructions next to the swatch.

Next, dry and iron the fabric, again according to the manufacturer's instructions. Remove any wrinkles and creases. Wrinkled fabric will not print evenly!

Before you print any repeat patterns on your fabric, you must find and mark the fabric's "grainline." As I've said, *crossgrain* refers to the horizontal threads that run perpendicular to the grain of your fabric. The crossgrain, or weft, wraps back onto itself at the edges of the fabric, creating the fabric's *selvage*. The selvage is the self-finished edge of the fabric, and it prevents the fabric from unraveling. *Grain* refers to the long, vertical threads (i.e., warp) of your fabric.

The threads of the grain are the strongest ones in your fabric, and clothing patterns are usually cut parallel to the grain so that the garment will be sturdy and won't pucker or twist when it is worn. Because most often you'll be cutting your fabric along the grain, you also want to print your repeat patterns in line with your fabric's grainline to ensure that your print will be even and will not appear lopsided or unevenly spaced once you've sewn it into a garment. There are three ways to find the grainline:

1. Make a small cut into the selvage on one side of your fabric **(see A)**, then tear your fabric along its width **(see B, C, D)**; it will naturally tear along the weft, or crossgrain. Because lightweight fabrics can snag easily, this method is only recommended for medium-weight fabrics, such as chambray. Don't force it: if your fabric does not tear easily, proceed to one of the other methods that follow.

Fold your fabric in half lengthwise (along the grain/warp, bringing the selvages toward each other), and align the folded sides by their torn edge **(see E)**. Your fabric should not look puckered or twisted. If it does, gently adjust your fold until your fabric lies completely flat. Iron along this fold to create a sharp crease. This crease is your grainline, and it will be a key reference for you as you print repeat patterns.

Tip

ALWAYS USE THE GRAINLINE, INSTEAD OF THE SELVAGE, AS A GUIDE WHEN PRINTING. ALTHOUGH THE SELVAGE MAY APPEAR TO BE STRAIGHT, IT IS USUALLY WOVEN MORE TIGHTLY THAN THE BODY OF THE FABRIC AND CAN SHRINK AT A DIFFERENT RATE THAN THE REST OF YOUR FABRIC.

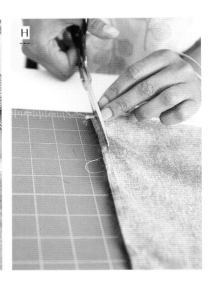

2. Another method is to remove a thread along your weft. To do this, cut into the selvage near one end of your fabric **(see F)**. Gently pull one of the weft threads away from the fabric **(see G)**. When you have pulled the thread out, cut along the line you just created by removing the thread **(see H)**.

Now, fold your fabric in half lengthwise (along the grain/warp, bring the selvages toward each other) and align the folded sides by the cross-grain line you just created **(see I)**. Make sure your fabric does not appear puckered or twisted, and iron along the fold to create the sharp crease that will mark your grainline.

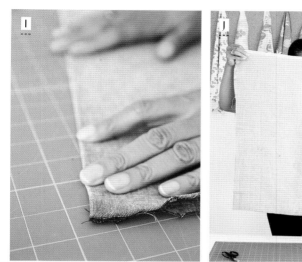

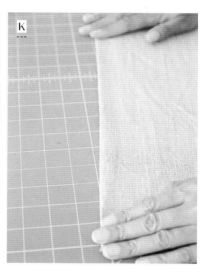

3. My favorite method, partly because it works well with the linen I love to use, is to fold the fabric in half lengthwise, lining up the selvages on both sides **(see J)**, and then to hold it up by the selvages and gently move them until the fold appears flat, without lumps or puckering. Flatten the fold line with your hand **(see K)**, then iron it. This fold line is your grainline. This works best with pieces of fabric that are two yards or less, as holding and adjusting larger pieces can get unwieldy.

BLOCK-PRINTING BASICS

I was a shy, anxious child, calmest when I was making things or reading. When I didn't have a book or a pencil in my hand, I focused my nervous energy on looking for patterns. And because shy kids spend a lot of time looking at the floor as a way of avoiding conversations, I spent a lot of time looking for patterns on the ground.

I found patterns everywhere: the parquet of my parents' den (squares pleasingly divided into four more squares, then subdivided into rectangular strips of wood), the hexagonal tile of my elementary school's bathroom, the uneven lines of the living room's hardwood floors. Even the neighborhood lawns, viewed up close, had patterns: clumps of clover and mallow interspersed among the grass.

My childhood anxiety prepared me well for a career as an artist. I've spent years finding visual patterns and mentally rearranging them. And even now, as a much calmer, more confident adult, I still find myself looking at the ground a lot, thanks to my small dog, Gus. Twice a day, every day, Gus and I go for a long walk in Golden Gate Park. While Gus busies himself with sniffing tree trunks and marking his territory, I'm looking at leaves and pods that have fallen to the ground—as well as all the shrubs, ferns, and flowers—and often these things find their way into my pockets for later inspection.

When I'm back in my studio, I draw the bits of flora I've picked up on my walks. I don't try to create realistic drawings; rather, I try to capture each item's essence, revealing just enough to evoke it. For example, an oak leaf's basic shape is instantly recognizable, and a California poppy can be represented through only the shape of its petals and the thin frilliness of its leaves.

Keeping a sketchbook is the most important part of my creative process. Actually, I have two sketchbooks: one that is small enough to fit in my purse and another, larger one that mostly lives in my studio. Both are tattered from use; neither is fancy or expensive. My sketchbooks are where I record what I see, develop my ideas, and make lots of mistakes. I also write in my sketchbooks, and I tape pictures, color swatches, and random items (such as leaves and flowers) in them. My sketchbooks serve as reference guides, too: so many times, I've used a sketch as a basis for a print months, or even years, after I created the original sketch.

Perhaps you've gathered all your tools and have selected your fabric, but you are nervous about creating your first design. You may think that you don't have any ideas, or you may believe that you can't draw. This isn't unusual; when I teach, I often have a student who panics at the sight of a blank piece of sketch paper. Truth be told, I often get nervous when I embark on a new project, feeling I have to start from scratch. But we rarely need to start from scratch. We all have opinions and specific tastes, and part of the creative process is figuring out how to translate those into a design.

When people tell me either that they have no ideas or that they can't draw, I suggest they start by keeping a sketchbook and repeatedly draw things that they like or are interested in. I tell them that it's important not to work too hard to find something to draw, and not to worry if an item seems too difficult to draw. The things we gravitate toward represent our own personal preferences. Also, the act of drawing something repeatedly increases our skills and helps shift our perspective; we start to understand our own points of view. In my case, my subsequent sketches of the same object often become simpler over time, as my perspective changes and I start to strip away what doesn't appear essential to me.

CREATING YOUR DESIGN

ALL MY PRINTS BEGIN AS SKETCHES IN MY SKETCHBOOK, and I rarely draw directly onto my block, preferring to work out my ideas with a pencil and paper instead. Using a sketchbook also allows me to visualize my final print, identifying and fixing mistakes before I start working on my block. Again, remember that the block will be the mirror image of your drawing and your final print. Unless you're exceptionally skilled, it is very difficult to draw a mirror image directly onto the block.

Often, my students want to rush through their drawings so they can begin carving and printing. And while it is true that much of the magic of block printing is in the printing itself, the art of the craft is embedded throughout the entire process. As you become more skilled, you can choose where in the process to economize; until then, take your time with each step and enjoy learning the craft.

DRAWING YOUR DESIGN

First, measure your block. Your image should be smaller than your block, and it's a good practice to leave ⅛ to ¼ inch of space between the outside of your image and the edge of the block, rather than have your image meet the edge of the block. For example, if you're using a 4 × 6-inch block, your image should measure no larger than 3¾ × 5¾ inches. When I teach, I recommend that my students begin by putting their block on their blank sketch paper and tracing around the perimeter of the block **(see A)**. Your image needs to fit comfortably within that box.

If you would like to create a two-color print, such as a flower whose petals and stem are two different colors, then you must create a separate block for each color. I discuss multicolor prints later in this chapter.

Next, you want to create an image that looks exactly the way you want your print to look. How you draw your image and indicate negative and positive space at this point are very important. It's important to use a consistent visual language when you're drawing and carving: items that are meant to print (the positive space) should be shaded in, and areas that are not meant to print (negative space) should be left blank. Make sure to keep your eraser handy—you'll probably have to do a bit of erasing at this point.

You may be tempted to rush this part of the process, preferring to draw just the outline of your image, not shading it in or erasing where necessary. However, I know from experience that cutting this corner will lead to mistakes once you start to carve. Setting up your drawing properly helps you to visualize the final print, and therefore will help you spot any potential problems before you transfer your image onto your block.

Your drawing skills will evolve as you do more and more printing. For your first print, you may want to start with a simple drawing that will be easy to execute. Then you can work your way toward more complex images. The more you print, the more you'll understand what you're capable of creating with the medium.

TRANSFERRING YOUR IMAGE

Now that you've created a design, transfer it to your block. To do this, place your tracing paper over your drawing **(see A).** Using a #2 or softer pencil, trace your drawing onto the tracing paper, making sure to shade it in exactly as you have on your sketch paper **(see B).**

Place your tracing paper face down on your block **(see C)**, so that the drawn-on side of your tracing paper is touching your block. Using your finger, rub the image **(see D).** This will transfer the graphite from your image onto your block. You can gently lift the edges of your tracing paper as you work to make sure that the image is transferring.

Once you have fully transferred your image, lift the tracing paper **(see E).** The mirror image of your design now appears on your block **(see F)**. If you'd like to make the image on your block darker, or if there are any places were the image didn't transfer well, use a permanent marker to fill in those areas. Your block is ready to be carved!

A

B

Tip

IF THE IMAGE ON YOUR BLOCK IS TOO LIGHT, YOU EITHER DID NOT USE ENOUGH PRESSURE WHEN TRANSFERRING THE IMAGE ONTO THE BLOCK, OR THE LINES AND SHADING ON YOUR TRACING PAPER ARE NOT DARK ENOUGH. IF THIS HAPPENS, SHADE YOUR TRACING PAPER AGAIN, THEN REPEAT THE TRANSFER PROCESS. YOU CAN USE THE OTHER SIDE OF YOUR BLOCK FOR THIS TRANSFER.

CARVING
YOUR
BLOCK

FIRST, CHOOSE A CARVING BLADE. I always recommend starting by carving the outline of your image, and a wider blade is usually best for this. Use the widest blade possible for the job. (For a refresher on the uses of the different blades, see page 6.)

Tip

PEOPLE OFTEN WANT TO START WITH THE SMALL V BLADE, WHICH IS THE SMALLEST AND WHICH DOES NOT WORK WELL ON THE SOFT BLOCKS WE'RE USING. THIS BLADE SHOULD BE RESERVED FOR CARVING FINE LINES.

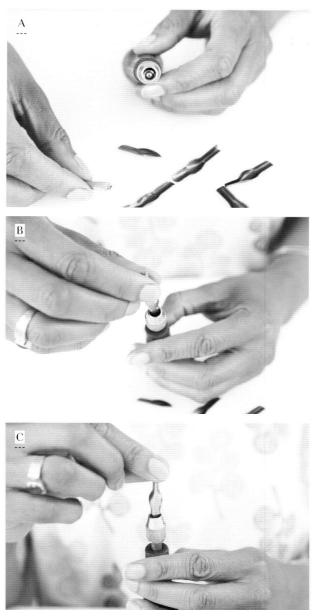

To insert the blade into your carving tool, loosen the metal band of the handle without unscrewing it completely. Look at the pieces that the metal band surrounds. There are two pieces: a metal ball in the center, and a small, U-shaped metal piece **(see A)**. Place the dull end of your blade in between the center metal ball and the smaller U-shaped metal piece **(see B)**. You should be able to insert the blade all the way to its shoulders without forcing it **(see C)**; if you cannot, loosen the band a bit more until the blade slides in smoothly. Tighten the band **(see D)**.

Tip

THE BLADE SHOULD NEVER TOUCH THE OUTER METAL BAND. IF YOU ARE HAVING PROBLEMS INSERTING THE BLADE, CHECK TO MAKE SURE THAT IT IS NOT LYING AGAINST THE METAL BAND RATHER THAN BETWEEN THE METAL BALL AND U-SHAPED METAL PIECE.

E
- - -

Tip

IT HELPS TO PRACTICE CARVING ON A PIECE OF SCRAP BLOCK FIRST. BEFORE WORKING ON YOUR GOOD BLOCK, USE SCRAPS TO FIGURE OUT WHAT WORKS FOR YOU: TRY OUT DIFFERENT BLADE SIZES, AND VARY THE AMOUNT OF PRESSURE YOU APPLY.

Your cutting tool is designed to fit comfortably into the palm of your hand **(see E)**. Turn your cutting tool so that the blade looks like a "U" or a "V." Rest your index finger on the metal band **(see F)**. This posture will help you create smooth, fluid lines and will prevent you from gouging or tearing your block while printing.

Start by carving the easiest areas, the ones with the least amount of detail. This is usually the outline of your image **(see G)** and the space around it. Remember that you'll be carving away anything that is not shaded in.

To carve, place your cutting tool almost parallel with the surface of the block **(see H)**. Do not carve at an angle— you may rip your block! Keeping your other hand out of the way, move your hand and cutting tool along the outline of your image, using enough pressure to carve at least ⅛ inch deep **(see I)**. There should be a visible difference between the height of the part of the block that will print, or the original surface, and the height of the part of the block that you do not want to print.

F

G

H

I

Tip

IF YOUR IMAGE IS ROUND OR HAS ROUND EDGES, ROTATE YOUR BLOCK AS YOU CARVE.

WHEN WORKING WITH IMAGES THAT HAVE SHARP CORNERS, START BY CARVING AWAY FROM, RATHER THAN INTO, THE CORNER. THIS WILL HELP YOU AVOID ACCIDENTALLY NICKING INTO THE CORNER.

Carve slowly, using fluid motions, and regularly check to make sure that you're holding your tool properly. One of the features of block prints is that the areas that aren't meant to print do print, revealing the carving lines and texture. For this reason, I'm deliberate about the direction in which I carve, carving in fluid lines that reflect the movement of my design so that if those lines do print, they add movement and energy to the overall design **(see J)**.

You may also want to cut away excess parts of your block, outside the rough outline of your image. This is particularly helpful when you will be printing repeat patterns and need to know where the edges of your image are. You can use an X-acto knife and a cutting mat to do this. Just remember to leave at least a ⅛- to ¼-inch border around your image when you cut your block **(see K)**.

If you are having a difficult time carving a smooth line or if you are ripping your block, you are probably holding your tool incorrectly, or your blade has become dull. Change out your blades as you go. Some areas, such as the background, may call for a wider blade. Other areas, such as interior details, will require you to use the #1 or #2 blade.

Continue carving until you've carved away any areas that aren't supposed to be shaded in and only the image you wish to print remains on the surface.

Try not to think too hard during the carving portion. Don't stop working every time you carve a new section, to research which blade you should use or which direction you should carve in. Rather, let the shape and movement of the image dictate the direction in which you carve and the blade sizes that you use. My decisions about blade size mostly come from experience and paying attention. Carving can be a meditative process. You just need to shut off all distractions and focus on the work in front of you.

A NOTE ABOUT MISTAKES

When I was learning to play the piano, my teacher always told me to continue playing when I made a mistake and not let the mistake fluster me. Later, in my high school figure-drawing class, we weren't allowed to use erasers. Instead, we learned either to live with our mistakes or, better, to listen to what they were telling us and incorporate them into our work.

In the same way, if you make a mistake when you're carving, let it be. Learn to work with it or work around it. Often, when you try to fix a mistake, you end up making it worse. Try embracing the handmade nature of your work, and learn from your mistakes. This is the only way to build your skills.

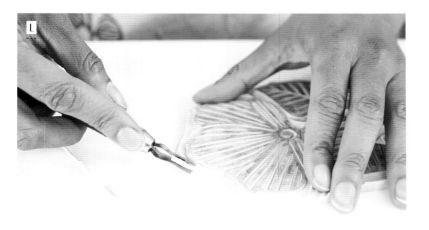

FINISHING YOUR BLOCK

Once you finish carving your block, you may be tempted to jump straight into printing. Don't! Instead, take a few minutes to tidy up your block to ensure that it has a clean, professional look. The neater your final block is, the neater your print will be.

If you haven't already trimmed away excess parts of your block, do so now. Just remember to leave at least ⅛ to ¼ inch between the border of your image and the edge of your block.

Next, bevel the edges of your block: carve a 45-degree angle around its edge **(see L)**. Beveling ensures that your fingers won't touch the inked portions of your block when you are printing.

Congratulations—you've carved your first block! Now you're ready to start printing.

PRINTING
ON FABRIC

THERE'S SOMETHING MAGICAL ABOUT PRINTING with a freshly carved block for the first time. All the work you've done thus far—from developing your design to spending hours carving your block—has led to this moment. Even after many years of printing, every single time I still look forward to making and seeing that first impression.

Take a few minutes to organize your printing station and make sure that you have all your printing tools at hand. Like carving, printing can be a meditative process. I don't like to interrupt my flow to search for a missing baren or jar of ink. And finally, because printing is a physical activity and requires you to spend a lot of time on your feet, make sure to wear comfortable shoes and stay hydrated.

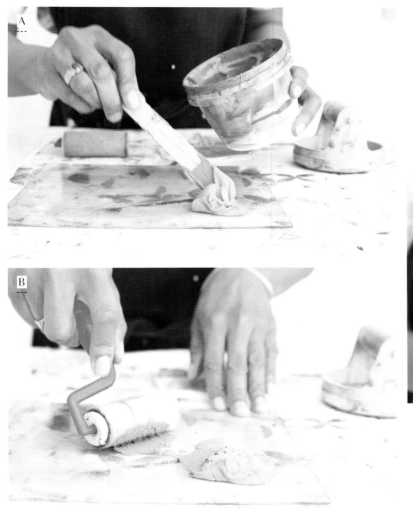

INKING AND TEST PRINTS

Using a spatula or a wooden stick, scoop out about a tablespoon of ink from the jar and place it onto a corner of your inking plate **(see A)**. Using your roller, roll a small amount of the ink from the corner into the center of your inking plate **(see B)**. Continue to roll the ink that you've placed in the center of your plate until there is a thin layer of ink on your plate and your roller is evenly coated. The ink you've rolled out on the plate should make a sticky sound when you roll it, and your roller should be evenly coated but not gloppy with ink **(see C)**. If you cannot see the texture of your roller cover under the ink, you are using too much ink. If your roller isn't coated enough, roll a bit more ink from the pile on the corner of your plate.

Next, gently roll the ink onto your block until your block is evenly coated **(see D).** Do not use pressure when you ink your block; this will force ink into the areas you do not want to print. You should still be able to see the printing surface of your block after you've inked it **(see E)**. If you cannot, then you've rolled on too much ink. If that is the case, simply wipe off your block, roll the ink out more thinly on your inking plate, and reapply to your block.

Lift your block and place it onto your test fabric. Press down on your block using either the palms of your hands **(see F)** (not your fingers—you can hurt your fingers that way!) or your baren **(see G)**. Move your hand or baren around to apply pressure to all parts of your block. Lift your block **(see H)**; you've done your first print!

You must reapply ink for every print **(see I)**. You may need to add more ink to the middle of your inking plate by pulling a bit more from the pile in the corner. As you print from your block repeatedly, you may find that ink begins to seep into fine lines and other areas of your block that you do not want to print. Use a towel, your fingernail, or the small end of a chopstick to remove it. In addition, lint and dust from your fabric may transfer onto your block and build up as you print. If this happens, wash your block with water and dry it, then continue to print. You also may need to replace your roller with a fresh, clean one partway through the process.

HEAT-SETTING YOUR PRINTS

Different brands of ink have different heat-setting requirements, and some become colorfast after a few days of air drying only. Always follow the manufacturer's instructions.

In general, allow the ink on your fabric to air dry until it is dry to the touch (usually overnight, though this can vary depending on your climate). Once it's dry, put the fabric in the dryer for a few minutes to remove any remaining moisture. Then, place a piece of muslin on top of your ironing board, then place your fabric, print side down, on top of it. Working in quadrants, iron the back side of your fabric for three minutes per quadrant. Do not use steam at this point; it may cause your ink to fade.

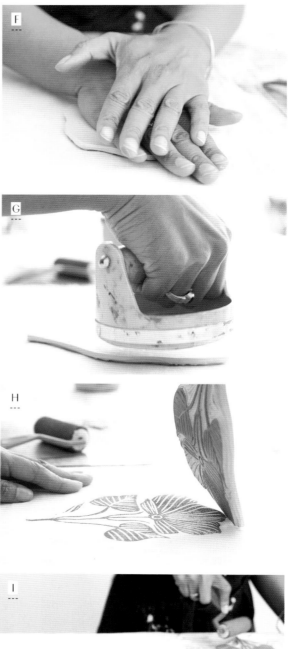

TROUBLESHOOTING PRINT PROBLEMS

Please don't expect mastery from the outset. You will encounter problems while carving and printing, especially in the beginning. You will probably apply too much ink or too much pressure, oversaturate your roller, or even print upside down. I've done all of these things many times. Part of the fun of block printing is experimenting to see what works for you, then making adjustments along the way. I have all of my prints from my "52 Weeks of Printmaking" project, so I can clearly see how, with all that practice, my carving and printing skills improved over the course of a year. Despite less-than-perfect prints at the outset, I kept block printing because I enjoyed it. That enjoyment got me through the early learning phase, when I created some rather ugly prints. While I was working my way through those prints, I was also developing my skills; at the end of the year, I had a visual record of how far I'd come.

That said, there are a few common mistakes that people frequently make when they're just starting out, and they are easily remedied:

Muddy print: *If your print is muddy, you have applied too much ink to your inking plate and roller. Either remove the ink by rolling the excess onto another inking plate, or replace the roller with a fresh, clean one.*

A faint print: *Faint prints usually arise when you have applied not enough ink to your block or not enough pressure while printing it. Experiment with ink coverage and pressure until you get the desired print density.*

Stray lines: *Stray lines are the result of either not carving the large negative areas deeply enough or applying too much pressure*

when you ink your block, thus forcing ink into the areas that aren't meant to print. In the case of the former, I usually let the stray lines stand. This effect is one of the hallmarks of block printing, and you will probably never get a perfectly clean print.

Ink pooling up around the edge of the print: *Check the edges of your block, and if this is where the excess ink is gathering, bevel them more. If the ink is pooling up around the edge of the image itself, carve the image more deeply, or use the carving knife to carefully cut away the area where the ink has been gathering.*

CLEANING UP

AFTER A LONG DAY OF MAKING, carving, and printing with your first blocks, you may want to put your feet up and relax, or you may want to just keep on printing. Before you finally call it a day, you must clean your tools and blocks. Because you're using nontoxic, water-based inks, it is safe to wash your materials in the sink, and cleanup is pretty easy.

WASHING AND STORING YOUR BLOCKS

You've spent a considerable amount of time creating your blocks. Spend some time cleaning them so that they will last a long time.

First, wash your blocks with warm water, dish soap, and a soft sponge. Don't use anything abrasive—this can alter the surface texture of your block or even scratch off bits of your block.

If there's ink nestled into the fine lines you've carved, use a chopstick or toothpick to clean out those nooks and crannies. Just be careful not to puncture the block. Then, towel it dry and lay it flat to air dry completely before storing.

I like to store my blocks in a box or a drawer. You can stack the blocks on top of each other, but separate each layer with a piece of tissue paper or tracing paper. Also, make sure that your block is completely dry before storing; otherwise, it may stick to the paper or to the other blocks.

WASHING YOUR INKING PLATE AND ROLLERS

Wash your inking plate with dish soap and a sponge. If the ink has dried a bit, soak it overnight first, or use a scouring pad.

If you're planning to use your rollers—and the same inks—again within 24 hours, you don't need to wash them right away. Just wrap them in plastic wrap and store in the freezer until you're ready to use them. The ink should stay fairly fresh.

It takes a little work to wash your rollers well. Once you've finished printing with them, rinse them a bit to get rid of excess ink, then soak them in water and a small amount of laundry detergent overnight. Rinse them out well and then let them air dry completely. Your rollers must be thoroughly dry before you can use them again, so make sure to buy a few replacement rollers if you're planning to make multicolor prints.

Your reused rollers will never be as pristine as when you bought them, but that's OK. They're showing signs of use, and that's a good thing.

PATTERN

DESIGNING AND PRINTING REPEAT PATTERNS

A repeat pattern is exactly what it sounds like: a design that is repeated in a regular manner to create a pattern. Most, if not all, commercially printed fabric utilizes repeat patterns, which are laid out digitally and then machine printed.

With a grid ruler and a little math, it's simple to create hand-printed repeat patterns. In this chapter, I'll show you the three most commonly used types of repeats: straight repeats, half-drop repeats, and bricked repeats.

Printing yardage is a time-consuming, physical process, but it can be an absorbing process, one in which you lose track of time. I make the most mistakes when I'm hungry and tired. Pay attention to your body while you print, and take breaks, stretch, and eat snacks when you need to.

THINKING WITH YOUR HANDS

Before I dive into the process of creating a carefully measured and plotted-out repeat pattern, I always play around on muslin. I like to do this printing free-form, experimenting with distances and direction and informally trying different patterns without worrying about measurements. Once I have something that pleases me, I'll note the measurements, direction, and type of repeat pattern. Then I'll print this pattern on a fresh piece of muslin, making small adjustments along the way and writing notes about measurements and offsets in my notebook, before I finally print on my good fabric.

I call this process "thinking with my hands," and it applies not just to repeat patterns but also to color. I may picture a particular print pattern in my head, but often it isn't until I've experimented on muslin a bit that the final print starts to reveal itself.

Don't be afraid to play with your prints. You won't know what's possible, and what works, until you've spent some time thinking with your hands.

OFFSETS

Before you start printing, it will be helpful to understand horizontal and vertical offsets, because I will make reference to them throughout the repeat pattern instructions.

Horizontal offset: This refers to the horizontal distance between the same sides, or reference points, of two objects. For example, if I say that the horizontal offset of two impressions in a pattern is 6 inches, that means that the left edge of the first impression is 6 inches from the left edge of the second impression. It would also follow that the center of the first impression is 6 inches from the center of the second impression.

Vertical offset: This refers to the vertical distance between the same sides, or reference points, of two objects. When I say that the vertical offset of two impressions in a pattern is 5 inches, that means that the top edge of the first impression is 5 inches from the top edge of the second impression.

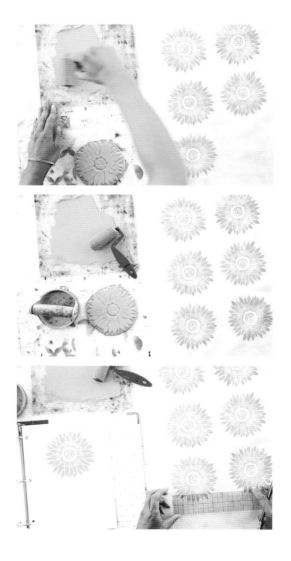

STRAIGHT REPEAT PATTERNS

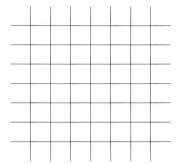

A STRAIGHT REPEAT PATTERN is the simplest pattern to create. It consists of an image—your block—printed in a grid, with evenly spaced rows and columns.

To create a straight repeat pattern, start by measuring your block. The block I'm using for this example is round, with a diameter of approximately 5 inches, meaning its height and its width are both 5 inches. Mark a center point of one side of your block on the back with a permanent marker to serve as your reference point for all measurements. Because my block is round, I marked the center bottom of the block **(see A)**. If you are using a rectangular block, mark either the center of the bottom edge of your block, or the left or right edge to serve as your reference point.

Next, figure out how much horizontal space and how much vertical space you want to appear between each impression. Again, I always recommend testing your pattern on inexpensive muslin first. If you have already tried out different variations on muslin, use the measurements of your favorite layout to create your final repeat pattern. To keep my print simple, I have decided to leave 1 inch, both horizontally and vertically, between each impression. This means that my vertical and horizontal offsets will both be 6 inches:

WIDTH OF BLOCK (5 INCHES)	HEIGHT OF BLOCK (5 INCHES)
+ HORIZONTAL DISTANCE BETWEEN IMPRESSIONS (1 INCH)	**+** VERTICAL DISTANCE BETWEEN IMPRESSIONS (1 INCH)
HORIZONTAL OFFSET (6 INCHES)	**VERTICAL OFFSET (6 INCHES)**

Tip

IT DOESN'T REALLY MATTER WHERE YOU MARK YOUR REFERENCE POINT, AS LONG AS YOU USE IT CONSISTENTLY WHEN YOU MEASURE AND PRINT.

A

Now that you have determined your measurements, it is time to prepare your fabric for printing. The length of your fabric will depend on the requirements of your sewing pattern. Mark the grainline of your fabric following the instructions on pages 14–17.

Now align the right edge of your grid ruler with the ironed grainline of your fabric. Check to make sure that the top edge of your ruler aligns with the weft of your fabric **(see B)**. This will ensure that you're printing on the grain of the fabric.

Decide where you're going to place your block, and make your first impression **(see C)**. Now you need to determine where to place your second horizontal impression. Because the reference point of my first impression aligns roughly with the 3-inch mark on my ruler, the reference point needs to align with the 9-inch mark for my second impression **(see D)**:

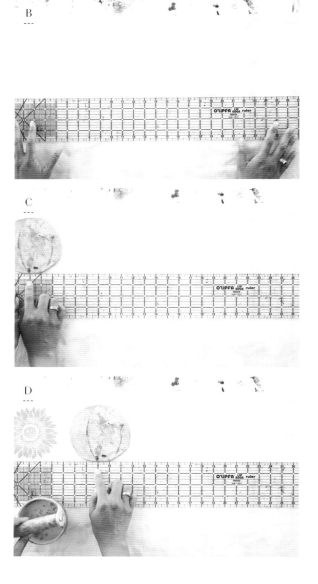

REFERENCE POINT OF FIRST
IMPRESSION (3-INCH MARK)

+ HORIZONTAL OFFSET (6 INCHES)

PLACEMENT OF REFERENCE POINT
FOR SECOND IMPRESSION (9-INCH
MARK)

By the same logic, the reference point will align with the 15-inch mark for my third impression on this row **(see E)**:

REFERENCE POINT OF SECOND
IMPRESSION (9-INCH MARK)

+ HORIZONTAL OFFSET (6 INCHES)

PLACEMENT OF REFERENCE POINT
FOR SECOND IMPRESSION (15-INCH
MARK)

Continue printing until you've completed the first row.

Tip I LIKE TO WORK IN QUADRANTS RATHER THAN PRINT THE WHOLE WIDTH OF MY FABRIC AT ONCE, BECAUSE MY FABRIC IS OFTEN WIDER THAN THE LENGTH OF MY RULER. I USE MY TAILOR'S CHALK TO MAKE MARKS INDICATING WHERE TO PLACE MY RULER WHEN I SWITCH FROM PRINTING ON ONE SIDE OF MY GRAINLINE MARK TO THE OTHER.

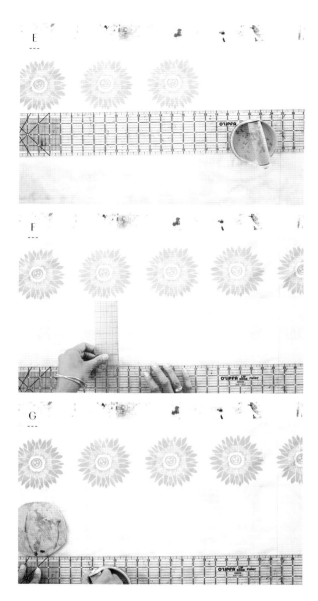

Next, create your second row. Remember: In this example, I am spacing out each impression by about 1 inch horizontally and vertically, so my vertical offset is also 6 inches. Measure the length of your desired vertical offset (6 inches in this example) down from the reference point of the first impression on the first row and place your grid ruler there **(see F)**.

Again, align the right edge of your grid ruler with the grainline of your fabric, and check to make sure that the top edge of your ruler aligns with the weft of your fabric. Print the second row in the same manner you printed the first, with the same horizontal offsets, so that you begin to create neat columns **(see G, H)**. Continue printing until you have completely filled your yardage **(see I)**.

Tip

YOUR RULER MAY NOT BE WIDE ENOUGH TO SPAN THE WIDTH OF YOUR FABRIC. IF THIS HAPPENS, USE TAILOR'S CHALK TO MARK YOUR GRAINLINE WHERE THE TOP OF YOUR RULER MEETS IT. THEN SIMPLY MOVE YOUR RULER OVER, ALIGNING THE TOP EDGE OF THE RULER WITH THIS MARK. MAKE SURE THAT YOUR RULER ALSO REMAINS ALIGNED WITH THE HORIZONTAL CROSSGRAIN OF YOUR FABRIC.

HALF-DROP REPEAT PATTERNS

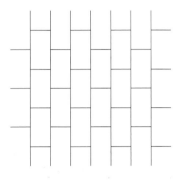

A half-drop repeat pattern is slightly more complex than a straight repeat. In a half-drop, your columns are still aligned; however, your rows zigzag, staggered by half a length of your block. If a straight repeat looks like a grid, a half-drop repeat looks a bit more like a set of stairs.

Measure your block. The block in this example is approximately 3 × 6 inches. Mark a reference point on the back of the block at the center of the bottom edge **(see A)**. For this print, I have decided on a ½-inch horizontal and vertical gap between each impression. Do the math to figure out your offsets:

WIDTH OF BLOCK (3 INCHES)

+ HORIZONTAL DISTANCE BETWEEN
IMPRESSIONS (½ INCH)

_____

HORIZONTAL OFFSET (3½ INCHES)

HEIGHT OF BLOCK (6 INCHES)

+ VERTICAL DISTANCE BETWEEN
IMPRESSIONS (½ INCHES)

_____

VERTICAL OFFSET (6½ INCHES)

A

Again, align the right edge of your grid ruler with the grainline of your fabric, ensuring that the top of your ruler runs parallel with the weft of your fabric. Decide where you're going to place your block, and make your first impression. In this example, I've placed the reference point at the 2-inch mark on the ruler **(see B, C)**. Now you need to determine where your next horizontal impression on this row will be. Since the second column will shift down by a half-step, you will skip printing the second column for now and leave that column empty. You will fill it in later.

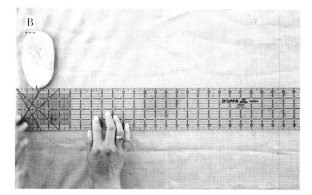

Let's do the math. Because the reference point of my first impression aligns roughly with the 2-inch mark on my ruler, my second impression on this row needs to align with the 5½-inch mark. This is a two-step calculation:

REFERENCE POINT OF FIRST
IMPRESSION (2-INCH MARK)

+ HORIZONTAL OFFSET (3½ INCHES)

**REFERENCE POINT IN SECOND
COLUMN (5½-INCH MARK)**

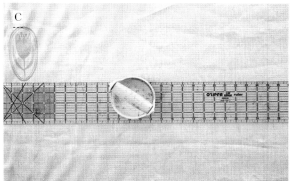

But remember: You're not printing the second column on this row right now; you will need to leave an empty column between each impression in this row to make space for the half-drop impression. So, the second step of this calculation is as follows:

REFERENCE POINT OF SECOND
COLUMN (5½-INCH MARK)

+ HORIZONTAL OFFSET (3½ INCHES)

**PLACEMENT OF REFERENCE POINT FOR
SECOND IMPRESSION (9-INCH MARK)**

So, for my second impression I need to align the reference point with the 9-inch mark on my ruler **(see D)**. The reference point of my first impression was at the 2-inch mark and the reference point of my second impression is at the 9-inch mark, so my horizontal spacing while actually printing will be 7 inches, or double the horizontal offset I calculated, to account for the column I am leaving blank. Continue printing until you have completed the first row **(see E)**.

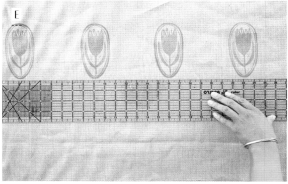

Next, print your second row. You've already determined your vertical offset (mine is 6½ inches), so measure down from the bottom of the first row and place your grid ruler there. Again, align the right edge of your grid ruler with the grainline of your fabric, checking to make sure that the top edge of your ruler aligns with the weft of your fabric **(see F)**. Print the second row in the same manner you printed the first, with the same horizontal offsets, so that you begin to create neat columns. Continue printing until you have completed the second row **(see G)**.

Now you're going to print the half-drop. Start by locating the reference point of your first impression. Next, you'll need to calculate the half-drop offset, which is half of the vertical offset:

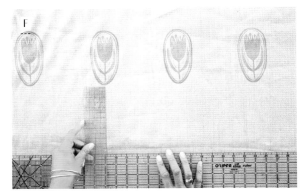

VERTICAL OFFSET (6½ INCHES)

÷ 2

HALF-DROP OFFSET (3¼ INCHES)

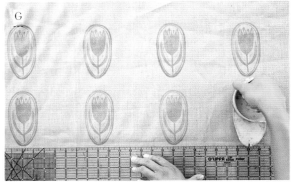

Measure the half-drop offset distance down from the reference point of one of the impressions in your first row. This is where you'll place your grid ruler **(see H)**. Print your first half-drop impression **(see I)**. You already did the math for where the reference point will land in the second column:

REFERENCE POINT OF FIRST IMPRESSION (2-INCH MARK)

+ HORIZONTAL OFFSET (3½ INCHES)

REFERENCE POINT IN SECOND COLUMN (5½-INCH MARK)

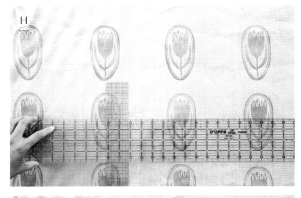

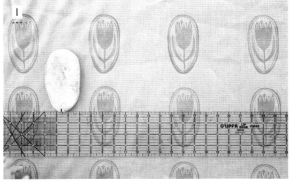

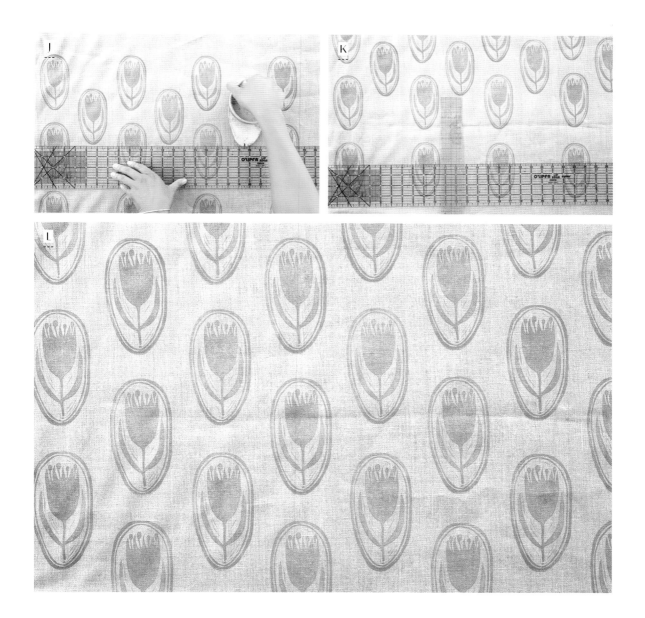

Remember that my horizontal spacing for actually printing is 7 inches, or double the horizontal offset, so my next impression on this row will be at 12½-inch mark on the ruler, and the next will be at 19½-inch mark. Continue printing until you've filled this offset row **(see J)**. To print the next offset row, measure down 6½ inches from the bottom of the previous half-drop row, and again align your grid ruler with the grainline of your fabric **(see K)**. Continue printing until you've filled your yardage **(see L)**.

BRICKED REPEAT PATTERNS

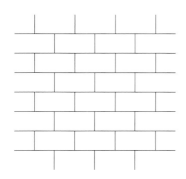

AS ITS NAME HINTS, A BRICKED REPEAT PATTERN is laid out the same way that bricks in a brick wall are. First, all the prints in the first row are evenly spaced, then the prints in the second row are shifted halfway to the right.

Again, measure your block and mark your reference point. The block in this example is approximately 5¼ x 7 inches. I have placed the reference point at the center of the bottom edge **(see A)**. Next, determine your offsets. For this print, I decided to keep a ¾-inch horizontal gap and a 1-inch vertical gap between impressions:

WIDTH OF BLOCK (5¼ INCHES)	HEIGHT OF BLOCK (7 INCHES)
+ HORIZONTAL DISTANCE BETWEEN IMPRESSIONS (¾ INCH)	**+** VERTICAL DISTANCE BETWEEN IMPRESSIONS (1 INCH)
HORIZONTAL OFFSET (6 INCHES)	**VERTICAL OFFSET (8 INCHES)**

A

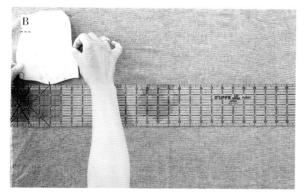

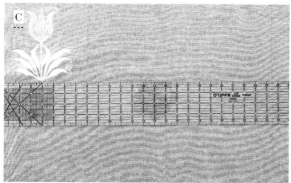

Align the right edge of your grid ruler with the grainline of your fabric, ensuring that the top of your ruler runs parallel with the weft of your fabric.

Decide where you're going to place your block, and make your first impression **(see B)**. Now you need to determine where to place your second impression. The reference point of my first impression is at the 4-inch mark on the ruler, so the reference point of my second impression needs to align with the 10-inch mark **(see C, D)**:

REFERENCE POINT OF FIRST IMPRESSION (4-INCH MARK)

+ HORIZONTAL OFFSET (6 INCHES)

PLACEMENT OF REFERENCE POINT FOR SECOND IMPRESSION (10-INCH MARK)

By the same logic, your third impression will align with the 16-inch mark **(see E)**:

REFERENCE POINT ON SECOND IMPRESSION (10-INCH MARK)

+ HORIZONTAL OFFSET (6 INCHES)

PLACEMENT OF REFERENCE POINT FOR THIRD IMPRESSION (16-INCH MARK)

Print to the end of the row.

To begin the second row, first measure the amount of your vertical offset down from the bottom of the first row **(see F)**, and place your grid ruler there. Align the right edge of your grid ruler with the grainline of your fabric, making sure that the top edge of your ruler aligns with the weft of your fabric.

Because this is a bricked pattern, the impressions on the second row will be shifted half a step to the right **(see G)**, so you will need to locate the first impression in the second row using half the horizontal offset. For example, the reference point of my first impression in the first row was at the 4-inch mark on the ruler. The horizontal offset is 6 inches, so half of the horizontal offset is 3 inches. This means my first impression in the second row should be at the 7-inch mark.

My horizontal offset for the rest of this row is still 6 inches, so the next impression on this row is at the 13-inch mark **(see H)**, and the following one will be at the 19-inch mark. Continue printing until you've filled this row **(see I)**.

To print the third row, measure down the amount of your vertical offset again (in my case, 8 inches), and again align your grid ruler with the grainline of your fabric. You will use the same measurements you used on your first row. Continue printing bricked rows until you've filled your yardage.

Congratulations—you've printed yardage! Allow the ink to dry, then heat-set your fabric using the instructions in chapter 2. Now you're ready to sew.

CREATING MULTICOLOR PRINTS

During art class in the first week of December when I was in fifth grade, my teacher passed out photocopied coloring sheets of Santa Claus and told the class the following: "Santa's coat and hat must be red, his boots can be black or gray, and you may use only black or white on his gloves." Ten-year-old me found this silly. After all, what's the point of an art class in which we're not allowed to be creative? I was a good kid, though, and complied, creating a Santa Claus who looked exactly like those of my classmates. Some artists talk about the teachers who encouraged them; instead, I remember the teachers whose constraints I fought against. Needless to say, I did not do very well in my elementary school art classes.

Free from fifth-grade restrictions, I am still not literal in my use of color. In my hands, a tree is just as likely to be pink as it is to be green or brown, and I probably use blues where nature never intended them to be. I love to play with color and come up with unexpected combinations. Here are a few different ways to combine colors in your prints.

TWO-COLOR PRINT WITH REGISTRATION

WHEN YOU PRINT AN IMAGE that will have more than one color—for example, a flower in which the stem and petals are different colors—you must print each color separately and ensure that each color meets or overlaps the other precisely. In printmaking, this practice of aligning colors is called "registration." If the colors aren't precisely aligned, they are said to be "out of register."

Most of my block-printed designs do not require precise registration. Even when they do, I'm not a stickler for perfection; I prefer the handmade look of slightly off-center prints. However, certain types of two-color prints do require some precision in order to work visually. Here's how to print a two-color—and therefore two-block—print using a flower and stem motif as an example.

Determine where you want the two blocks to align and which block you'll print first. For this design, I have decided to print the stem first so I can align the bottom of the flower with the top of the stem, which I think will be easier. Find the point on your second block where you want it to meet a certain point on the first prints you've already made, and mark the front and back of the block. I am marking the bottom center of the flower block where I want it to meet the stem **(see A)**. Cut away the excess block at the point you marked (that is, re-move the margin between the image and the edge of the block) so that the image meets the edge of the block just at that point **(see B)**. This will help you to see where to line up the second impression.

Tip

EACH COLOR NEEDS ITS OWN SEPARATE BLOCK; DO NOT USE MULTIPLE COLORS ON THE SAME BLOCK AT THE SAME TIME. THERE ARE A FEW REASONS FOR THIS: DIFFERENT INK COLORS REQUIRE DIFFERENT AMOUNTS OF PRESSURE TO PRINT EVENLY; IT IS VERY DIFFICULT TO KEEP THE DIFFERENT COLORS OF INK ON THE SAME BLOCK SEPARATE FROM EACH OTHER; AND SOME EFFECTS—FOR EXAMPLE, LAYERING DIFFERENT COLORS ON TOP OF EACH OTHER—ARE IMPOSSIBLE TO CREATE USING JUST ONE BLOCK.

Print the first block **(see C)**. Ink the second block, then align the point marked on the back of the block with the appropriate point on the printed image. In this example, I am aligning the mark at the bottom center of the flower block with the top of the stems **(see D)**. Because the excess block under the center point has been cut away, the flower block rests directly above the stem **(see E, F)**. When printing in this way, you may have to eyeball the placement of the second impression and make a few adjustments as you go, which is why I recommend printing your yardage of your first block before inking and printing the second one.

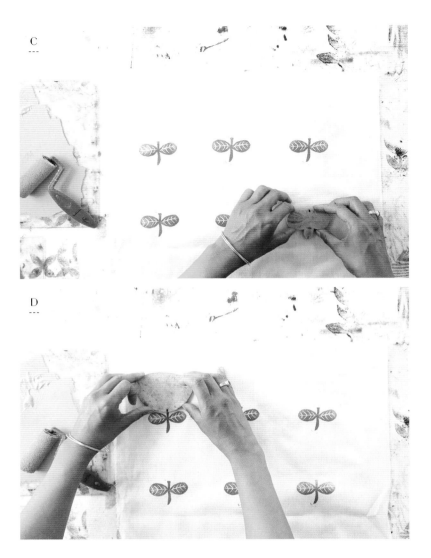

C

D

E

F

To calculate offsets for a repeat pattern with two blocks, use the dimensions of the whole image—in this case, the flower and stem combined. Then use these whole-pattern offsets while printing the first block. Measure and print all the yardage with the first block first. You won't need to measure out where to place the second block, because its placement is already dictated by the placement of the first.

SAME BLOCK, ALTERNATING COLORS

A MUCH EASIER WAY TO INTRODUCE A SECOND COLOR into your prints is to use the same block but alternate colors. You can alternate colors every other row or column, or place the second color randomly.

You will need to wash and dry your block before switching to another color, so print all of one color first, leaving gaps wherever the second color will be placed, then clean your block. Once your block is dry, you can switch to your second color.

LAYERED MULTICOLOR PRINT, NO REGISTRATION

ADDING SPOTS OF COLOR RANDOMLY IS THE EASIEST WAY to add a second color. In this example, I printed the pink dots first, placing them randomly **(see A)**. I then used a precise half-drop repeat pattern to layer a second color—the floral motif—on top **(see B, C)**.

When you do this, let your ink dry before applying the next color. Otherwise, the ink from the first color can transfer to the block when you are printing the second color.

BLOCK PRINT GALLERY

The prints in this book reflect my love of flora and landscapes, both the real ones from my daily walks through Golden Gate Park and the ones I've made up in my head. In this chapter, I include information about the creation of each print. Templates for all the prints featured in this book are available beginning on page 149.

Please don't fret if your work doesn't look exactly like mine. Your work is a reflection of you; you will bring different experiences, skills, and points of view to your prints than I bring to mine.

And don't limit yourself to using only my designs. These are merely meant to be a starting point for you; draw, experiment, and create work that appeals to your own specific tastes and ideas!

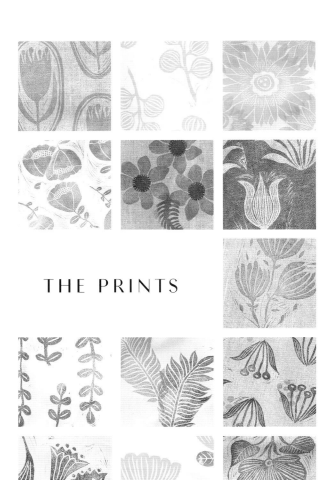

THE PRINTS

POPPY

ANEMONE

This is one of the simplest blocks in the book, requiring little detailed carving. I left the block rectangular, rather than trimming along the outline of the image, because I knew I wanted to use it in a straight repeat pattern. I also incorporated the carve lines into the print, which mirror the movement of the image. With a minimal amount of carving, it makes a fantastic beginner block, and it pairs well with the Square Scarf pattern (page 93).

Anemones and ranunculus are my two favorite flowers. Others may love peonies and roses, but my tastes are far less pedigreed. These flowers always remind me of the winter of 1995, when I was twenty and living in Paris for a semester abroad. It hadn't occurred to me until I lived in France to buy my own flowers, and to buy them every week. But these anemones were sold for 25 francs (about five dollars back then) at every corner flower stand. I always found enough money in my student budget to buy a bunch.

Whenever my new friends visited my tiny studio for "un cocktail" or for a dinner of cashew chicken or ginger rice soup (the only two dishes I could prepare at that time), they would bring me a small bouquet of anemones. When I realized that buying and receiving flowers was a part of my temporary Parisian life, I went to the market to buy a vase—the very first one I would ever buy myself.

This print isn't a repeat pattern. Rather, for this print I placed the images randomly, preferring a more spontaneous layout to evoke a bouquet of flowers. And since I planned to use this fabric on the Foldover Clutch project (page 116) rather than on a garment, I wasn't concerned with aligning the prints with the grainline.

SEED PODS

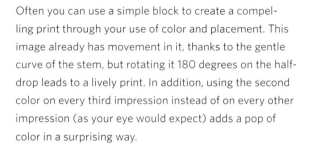

Often you can use a simple block to create a compelling print through your use of color and placement. This image already has movement in it, thanks to the gentle curve of the stem, but rotating it 180 degrees on the half-drop leads to a lively print. In addition, using the second color on every third impression instead of on every other impression (as your eye would expect) adds a pop of color in a surprising way.

WILLIAM MORRIS FLOWER

This flower is an homage to William Morris, a British textile designer and one of the founders of the Arts and Crafts movement. His textile work, which centers on stylized representations of the natural world, has greatly influenced me.

Like William Morris's botanical prints, this block is large, measuring more than 4 × 6 inches. I prefer to use large blocks when creating fabric for garments that require a lot of yardage, such as full skirts and dresses. Not only do bigger blocks make printing large amounts of fabric easier (because the block covers a larger area of fabric, it requires fewer impressions to fill the fabric), but they also pack a big visual punch.

I spaced the vertical offsets for this print to make the flowers appear to be connected in a continuous vertical line, and then rotated the half-drop to create a nondirectional print. Fabric with a directional print has a distinct top and bottom, while fabric with a nondirectional print does not. This means that you can place your pattern pieces on your fabric and not have to worry about laying them out in the same direction as the print.

STICKY MONKEY FLOWER

OLIVE BRANCH

Yes, there really is a plant named "sticky monkey." It's a California native plant, and it gets half of its name from its sticky leaves and the other half from its flowers, which look like a monkey's face viewed head on. I first saw this plant growing wild when I was at sleepaway camp. The name sounded so funny to seven-year-old me that I'm still able to identify the shrub and flower all these years later.

Summer camp was also where I first learned the names of native plants—not just the ubiquitous California poppy but also Indian paintbrush, Manzanita, and madrones. Decades later, I simultaneously impress and bore my friends when I point out these plants on hikes.

Although this print looks like it's made from two separate blocks, it's actually made using one 4 × 6-inch block, printed in a half-drop repeat pattern with a 180-degree rotation on the half-drop. The lines that I created around the flower image were not part of my sketch, but I knew that I wanted to include some background movement to add depth to the image. I was very deliberate about how I carved the block, carefully carving in a way that would mirror the overall movement of the image.

Olive trees are low maintenance and easy to grow in Mediterranean climates, which is probably why they line the sidewalks in my San Francisco neighborhood. The simple, iconic shape of the olive's leaves and branches also makes easy-to-carve images and simple, pretty prints. While these blocks look great printed on their own, I also like to use them for border prints or mixed with other blocks to create layered, more complex prints.

FERNS

DAHLIA

I grew up in a house filled with ferns, which is noteworthy because these tropical plants aren't supposed to grow well in Southern California's hot, dry climate. But my mom has always had a way with houseplants, and she somehow managed to get these finicky plants to thrive and multiply. In fact, the ferns currently in my parents' house are direct descendants of the ferns of my childhood.

This print uses two blocks, adding visual interest by layering two related colors on top of each other. Here I've printed them in two shades of green on white for a summery, tropical feel; in the fall, you could try it in darker shades on an oatmeal-colored linen, for example.

On our daily walk to the park, Gus and I pass a small church with a front garden that is tended to by one of the church's elderly congregants. Summer through early fall, the garden is filled with large, lush dahlias. From June to October, dahlias provide the bursts of color that are often missing during San Francisco's dreary, foggy summers—which is probably why it has been adopted as the city's official flower.

Here I have created a two-color print. I printed the first color in a straight repeat pattern, then I overlaid the second color on top, shifting this layer halfway to the right and halfway down. The result is a layered print that looks much like a dahlia garden in the summer. The amount of detail in this block makes it appear far more difficult to carve than it actually is. Just be sure to use a sharp blade on the fine lines.

SCANDINAVIAN BLOOM

CAMEO TULIP

I love the clean, neutral look of modern Scandinavian interior design. It's a look that I've tried—and failed—to implement in my own life, because I'm unable to show restraint when it comes to colors and patterns in my home. But then there are Scandinavian textiles! I adore the bold prints and saturated colors of Marimekko and Josef Frank textiles as well as the whimsy of traditional folk patterns.

This two-color flower evokes Scandinavian folk patterns while its muted, pastel colors reflect the calm of a minimalist interior. Of course, it would also look great in a more traditional palette of red and green.

On my eighteenth birthday my mom gave me a set of Victorian cameo jewelry, which my grandmother had purchased on her first trip to Italy. Included in the set was a ring that was set with a large silhouette of a woman. I loved that ring, and wore it almost every day for twenty years before I lost it. The cameo silhouette is one of my favorite motifs, and it inspired the logo for my business.

I've found that almost any simple image, such as this quirky tulip illustration, is made instantly fancier by adding a border around it. I printed it in a directional, half-drop repeat pattern to evoke a Victorian wallpaper design.

CALIFORNIA SPICEBUSH

TURKISH TULIP

When hiking, you usually smell the California spicebush before you see it. As its name suggests, it smells like allspice—or like red wine. It's a pretty plant, with bright green leaves and beautiful red flowers. And while my color use is rarely literal in my botanical prints, I gladly made an exception for the spicebush, printing it in its lovely magenta.

I used a nondirectional, half-drop repeat pattern for this print, so that I would not have to think about matching up the images at the seams, or worry about the impressions on the straps appearing upside down.

On vacation in Istanbul, I saw stylized representations of tulips everywhere. Turkey is a textile lover's paradise, and images of tulips, which probably made their way to Western Europe through what is now Turkey, appear in lots of Turkish ornamental art.

This design is a simplification of the ornate traditional Turkish tulip image. I printed it in white ink on blue cotton chambray to give the timeless motif a new, modern look.

CROCUS

I like to use small prints like this for fabric destined for smaller items, such as bags or shoes. Large prints tend to lose their impact when fabric is cut small, but the scale of a smaller print allows the full image to remain visible even after the fabric has been cut into small pieces. Using a small block for a repeat pattern also means making more impressions per yard, though, which can make printing enough fabric for a larger project tiring.

The main image of this print—the crocus plant—was printed as a half-drop repeat pattern. However, the pink dots that make up the background image were printed randomly. I did this to give the print a bit of whimsy and movement, since I intended to use the fabric for a pair of espadrilles.

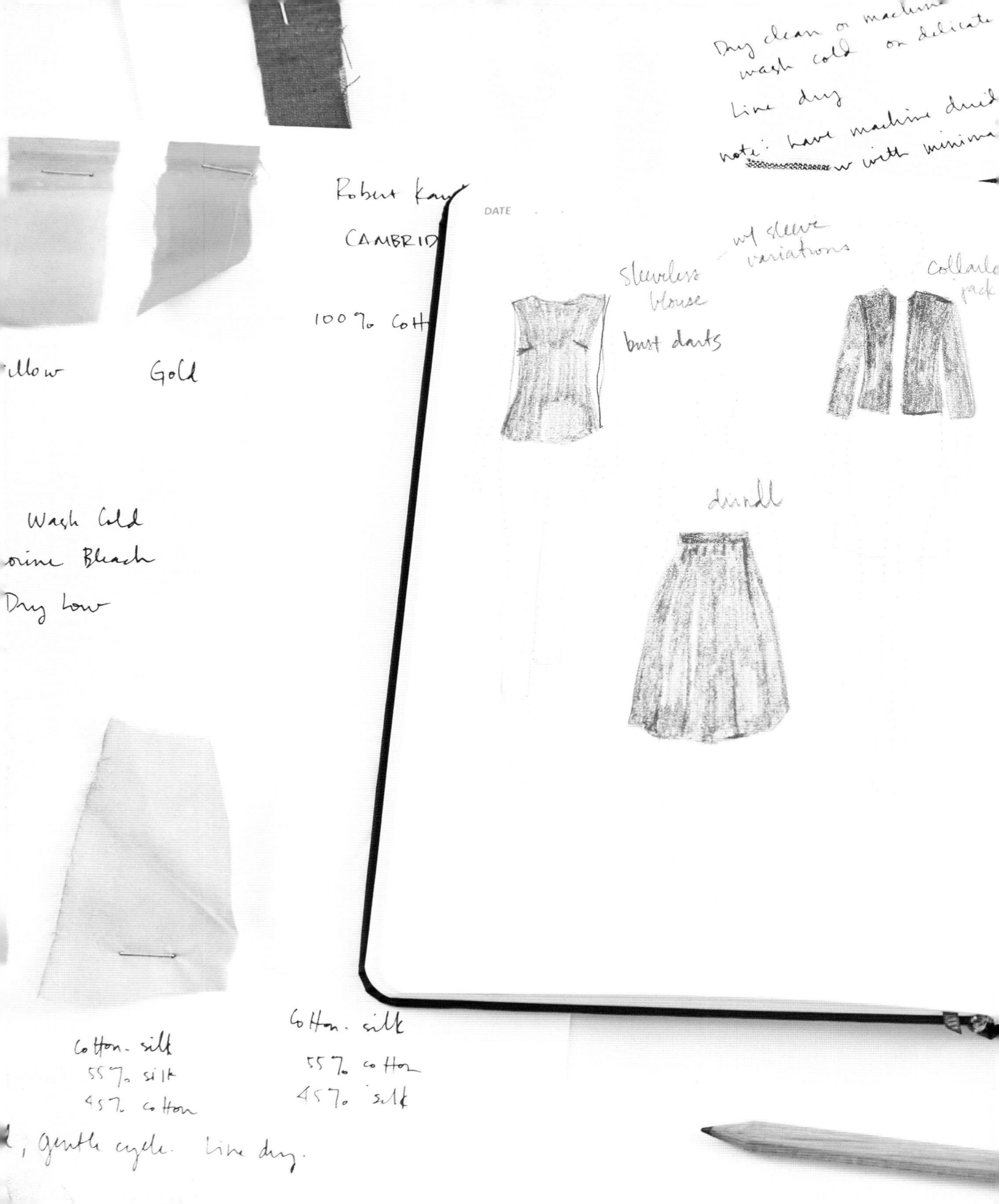

Dry clean or machine
wash cold on delicate
line dry
note: have machine dried
w with minimum

llow   Gold

Robert Kaye
CAMBRID

100% Cott

sleeveless
blouse

w/ sleeve
variations

bust darts

Collarle
jack

dirndl

Wash Cold
rine Bleach
Dry Low

Cotton- silk
55% silk
45% cotton

Cotton- silk
55% cotton
45% silk

l, gentle cycle. Line dry.

Bust darts?

Boat neck
Pockets
full skirt

also variation
of sleeves

Your appearance is the
first thing you say to
somebody.   HONY

SEW

THE *PRINT, PATTERN, SEW* WARDROBE

There is nothing fussy about the clothes I sew. You'd think that, considering my twelve years of wearing a boring Catholic school uniform, I would run toward ruffles, sparkles, and frills. But instead I've adopted a new uniform of sorts: simple, well-cut silhouettes made more vibrant through the use of bold prints and quality fabrics.

Even though I work at home, where I could wear my pajamas all day if I wanted to, I prefer to get dressed for work every day. I like to signal that my workday is beginning; after many years of working in offices for other people, getting dressed still puts me in a work mind-set. Most of the time you'll find me wearing jeans and a brightly colored shirt, if I plan to print that day, or a full skirt with a fitted shirt if I'm not planning to do any messy work. I prefer that my dresses not have too many fastenings or princess seams that would break up my prints. Scarves are a must, even in summertime, as San Francisco summers are notoriously cold. And finally, all skirts and dresses must have pockets for storing keys and dog treats, and for collecting leaves and twigs on my walks.

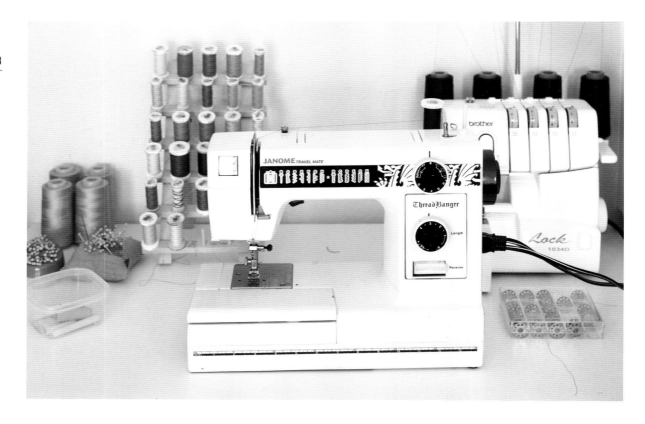

My wardrobe also takes into consideration my own attitude toward sewing. Although I'm an intermediate-level sewer, I still prefer garment patterns that take just a few hours to complete. I'd much rather spend time printing!

In the same way that I never use ink straight out of the jar, preferring to mix custom colors instead, I rarely use sewing patterns exactly as directed. I'm often attracted to the possibility of a pattern: the silhouette of a dress whose hem I will lengthen, or the fit of a dress whose neckline I plan to alter. I've even drafted patterns that are mash-ups of patterns I've purchased, to create exactly the garment I want.

When it came time to create the clothing patterns for this book, I knew that my pattern drafting skills were not good enough for the task. Instead, I decided to work with Barrie Brouse and Kenny Liang, who have created patterns for some of my favorite brands. They combined my rough sketches and mood boards with their expertise. My first directive was that they create patterns that reflect my own style: simple, timeless shapes that are fitted without being restrictive.

My second request was that the garments be easy enough for an advanced beginner sewer to make.

The results are even better than I had imagined. When Barrie dropped off the first samples, I gasped. The samples were so beautiful even in their plain, unprinted fabric, that I knew they'd be incredible once I'd remade them with my own fabric. Luckily, I was the fit model, so all the samples were in my size!

THE PATTERNS

WHEN I STARTED SKETCHING IDEAS for the garments in this book, I kept returning to the idea of a uniform. I knew I wanted to create a collection of basic staples that would work well with each other and with the type of clothes I already owned. I looked to my own wardrobe to figure out what I wore most often, and I developed my sketches around those pieces.

The result is this collection of versatile garments that can be worn together or with the basics already in your wardrobe. I purposely designed a skirt that works just as well with a plain T-shirt as with a structured blazer, and a coat that looks great both with jeans and with a dress. None of these garments and accessories should be saved for special occasions; incorporate them into your everyday wardrobe to add a splash of color and pattern to your life.

SCARVES

I was twenty when I first started wearing scarves. I'd moved to Paris for a study abroad program, and had just one suitcase's worth of clothes to last me six months (because I'd worn a school uniform for twelve years, packing that little wasn't difficult). Scarves weren't that common in warm, sunny Los Angeles, but they were a big deal in Paris—and they turned out to be a perfect, inexpensive way to add color and variety to my small wardrobe. These days, my printing uniform consists mainly of well-worn jeans and three-quarter-sleeve shirts—clothes I don't mind getting dirty—with a hand-printed scarf to liven things up.

COAT

SHORT-SLEEVED DRESS

This coat is one of the most versatile garments I own. On printing days, I wear it to cover my casual, ink-splattered clothes when I venture outside, but I also often pair it with a dress or a skirt on occasions when I want to look more dressed up. Whatever the outfit, this coat always makes me look more put-together.

The beauty of a dress is that it's an instant outfit. You put on that one piece of clothing and a pair of shoes, and you're done. As a fancier, woven version of a T-shirt dress, this dress scores bonus points for being both polished and comfortable.

SHORT-SLEEVED BLOUSE

CAP-SLEEVED DRESS

A boxy, pull-on blouse is one of the first things I learned to sew. It's a garment that is easy to make, and with its easy fit and flattering neckline, it is even easier to wear. I often pair this with jeans to work in my home studio, or dress it up with a skirt when an occasion calls for less casual attire.

I rarely sew (or buy) dressy clothes, because I want to own things that can be worn daily. I'd thought I'd include this vintage-feeling dress as an exception, but I've ended up wearing it so much—in both printed and plain fabric—that I've decided it's a staple.

CAP-SLEEVED BLOUSE

FULL SKIRT

I didn't plan to have this pattern made, but then I liked the fit of the cap-sleeved dress so much that I asked Kenny to create a blouse pattern based on that dress's bodice. It dresses up jeans and also pairs well with the coat and the full skirt.

I could live in this skirt. Actually, I do live in this skirt! It is just so comfortable, and it has pockets—two key requirements for my daily uniform. If you're nervous about wearing prints, this skirt is a great way to introduce pattern into your wardrobe. Wear it with a solid-color fitted top if you're print-shy, or mix it with the cap-sleeved blouse if you're ready to make a statement with prints. It also looks great paired with the coat.

ESPADRILLES

I had no idea that I could make my own espadrilles until I noticed a few of the French sewing bloggers I follow on Instagram doing just that. I ordered a pair of espadrille soles and sewing supplies from a fabric store, rummaged through my scrap bin, and spent an afternoon assembling the cutest pair of summer shoes.

APRON

I always wear aprons, even when I'm not printing or working around the house. Originally, I did this to protect my clothes from the dog hair that inevitably ends up covering everything I own, but I quickly grew to love the way a brightly printed apron adds a pop of color and pattern to even the plainest of outfits. These days, aprons are so much a part of my wardrobe that I have to remind myself to take my apron off before I go outside!

CROSS-BODY BAG

FOLDOVER CLUTCH

I love the way cross-body bags look, but they often have thin straps that are uncomfortable to wear once the bag is full. I designed this bag with a wide, soft strap for comfort and made the bag itself large enough to hold my sketchbook and pencils, for those days when I draw in the park or ride my bike to the beach.

The very first printed textile pieces I ever made and sold were zippered bags. I still make them, and their sizes and designs have varied over time. My current favorite is this big foldover clutch. I always pack one of these when I travel: I can slide my laptop or papers into it, then use it in lieu of an evening bag for dressier events. I think of clutches as statement pieces, making them a great way to incorporate bright colors and large patterns into my wardrobe.

TOTE BAG

A friend once told me, embarrassed, that he might have a tote bag problem. "I have so many tote bags. I can't help myself," he confessed. I responded that I didn't think it was a problem at all, that I probably had a dozen bags that I had bought or made over the years.

When I got home, I counted my collection, and I learned that I had far more than a dozen bags. I had made many of the bags myself, using pieces of my fabric that weren't large enough for clothes but weren't small enough to justify throwing away (although, let's be honest: I rarely throw any of my fabric away). I still contend that having a large stash of tote bags isn't a problem; they have so many practical uses.

MIXING PRINTS

I PROBABLY FIRST COMBINED PRINTS when I was four years old and dressing myself for the first time, but didn't start doing it again until I became a printmaker. Even then, I combined different patterned textiles only in the small bags and pouches I made. Eventually, inspired by designers such as Duro Olowu and Dries Van Noten, the pattern play in my bags spilled over into my wardrobe.

I recently listened to an interview with the fashion designer Isaac Mizrahi. He said, "How do you know if two prints work together? Like, a print and a stripe? Here's how you know: if you like it. If you like it, darling, it's right."[1] I suspect a lot of people want to mix prints and colors—and already know what they like—but they refrain from doing so because they don't want to look like a four-year-old who's just started dressing herself (but who probably has more natural confidence than most grown-ups!). Or perhaps they think that mixing prints is difficult to do well. I learned mainly through trial and error. If you are shy about mixing and matching prints in your own wardrobe, here are a few suggestions for getting started:

1 Isaac Mizrahi, Debbie Millman, *Design Matters with Debbie Millman*. March 2, 2015. www.debbie-millman.com/designmatters/isaac-mizrahi.

◄ **Start with accessories:** If you're shy about wearing a lot of pattern, start with your accessories. A colorful tote bag or a printed scarf nicely accentuate an outfit that includes a print. Just don't make them too matchy-matchy, or you may end up looking like you're wearing a uniform.

▲ **Keep everything in the same color family:** The print for this skirt is in the same blue as in the blouse's print. Even though the prints are very different, the outfit looks cohesive because the colors match.

Use the same print but in different colors: This is when printing your own fabric comes in really handy. Use the same block and layout to print two different fabric yardages, each in a different color.

▲ **Wear a large, bold print and a more subtle secondary print:** Think of men's suits and ties. Suits are often made in a textured fabric with a subtle, tonal pattern (often, stripes or plaid) and are worn with a patterned shirt and a vibrant tie. Adapt this to your own wardrobe, wearing a bright statement piece alongside subtle patterns that don't call attention to themselves.

Play with scale: Enlarge or reduce one of your block designs to create blocks of the same image in different sizes. For example, you can print coat fabric using the larger block and dress fabric using the smaller block. To make your outfit even more interesting, without looking too madcap, print them in different colors of ink or on different-colored fabric.

Of course, you don't have to wear all your printed clothes at the same time. Wearing just one boldly patterned garment in an otherwise neutral outfit can be just as striking as wearing patterns from head to toe.

CARING FOR YOUR HAND-PRINTED WARDROBE

You might be tempted to save your hand-printed clothes for special occasions, locking them away so they don't get dirty or damaged or ruined from wear. But don't put them away! Clothes are meant to be worn, and life is too short not to wear the pieces that you love. I'd like to caution you against treating your hand-printed garments as precious items.

The natural fibers I like to print on and sew with tend to soften with wear and laundering. They will never again look as crisp and new as they did the first time you wore them, but that's not the point. Clothes—even handmade clothing—are meant to be lived in. With some care, your clothes will last and become even more beautiful with age.

LAUNDERING AND IRONING

Once your fabric has been heat-set, the print will be largely colorfast. You can now wash and dry your fabric according to the manufacturer's instructions. However, do not use bleach or any harsh solvents to clean your fabric, as these may fade your prints. I prefer to use a gentle fragrance- and color-free detergent. Iron your garments when they are dry or still damp. You can also now use steam on them; the steam won't fade the ink on heat-set prints.

A NOTE ABOUT COLORFASTNESS

I say that heat-setting your fabric makes it "largely" colorfast because colors will still fade a bit in the first couple of washes, some of the more vibrant colors more than the others. Yellows, for example, tend to fade more than browns. Some mild fading is to be expected; don't fret about it too much, and instead embrace the handmade nature of your creations!

SEWING PROJECTS

I find it really tough to walk by a fabric store without stopping in and buying something. As a result, I always seem to have a stash of store-bought fabric waiting for just the right project. However, I am way more deliberate in how I use my hand-printed fabric. Often, I have a garment or a project in mind before I start printing yardage.

The following projects will help you put your hand-printed fabric to use. Some require as little as half a yard, while others call for over two yards. Take some time to read through each project's fabric requirements before starting to print so that you'll be sure to print enough.

Seam allowance: A seam allowance is the distance between the raw edge of your fabric and the sewn seam. Unless otherwise noted, all the projects in this book use a ½-inch seam allowance.

Edgestitch: An edgestitch is a functional stitch that is less than ¼ inch from the outer edge or seam of the fabric. It is usually not meant to show on the outside of a garment. An example of an edgestitch is the line of stitches used to sew fabric to a regular zipper.

Topstitch: A topstitch is similar to an edgestitch in its uses, but it is meant to show on the outside of a garment and it is typically more than ¼ inch from the edge of the outer edge or seam of the fabric. An example of a topstitch is a garment hem.

Understitch: An understitch is an edgestitch that is most often used to prevent the edges of fabric from rolling out and showing on the right side of the fabric. It's most often used on faced necklines and armholes, as well as under lapels and collars.

Basting stitches: Basting stitches are wide, loose stitches that are made to temporarily hold garment pieces together until you make your permanent stitches. They are also used to hold pleats and create gathers in skirts. To sew basting stitches, adjust your machine's setting to the lowest tension and the longest stitch length. Sew as directed, without backstitching at the beginning or end of your row of stitches.

Seam finishing: *Finishing* refers to the way you finish the raw edges of your fabric once it's sewn so that the edges will not unravel when washed. The most common ways to finish seams are by using a serger or overlock machine or by making a zigzag stitch with your sewing machine. On more delicate fabrics, such as cotton-silk blends, handkerchief linen, and cotton voile, you may instead choose to use French seams while sewing your garment. French seams are a way to completely encase a raw edge within another seam, and they require some advance planning to execute correctly. You can also use pinking shears to finish your seams, but pinked seams do not have the longevity that serged seams do.

Fusible interfacing: Interfacing is a type of fabric used to give the fabric it is bound to some stiffness. *Fusible* means that you attach it to your fabric by ironing. It's often used in facing and waistbands. Unless the directions instruct you otherwise, use interfacing of the same weight as your fabric, and follow the manufacturer's instructions to fuse it to your fabric.

Clipping: *Clipping* refers to the small, vertical cuts you make into the seam allowance of a concave curve to let the seam allowance spread out and lie flat when your garment is turned right side out. Clipping is often used on necklines and armholes. Clip at even intervals—usually ½ inch will suffice—and be careful not to clip into your stitches.

All these sewing projects require:

Sewing machine with a regular presser foot

Tailor's chalk

A ruler

Pins

Scissors or rotary cutter

Any additional tools that are required for a project are noted in that project's "Materials and Tools" list.

	SIZE (US)	XS	Small	Medium	Large	XL
SIZE CHART	*BODY MEASUREMENT (in inches)*					
	BUST	30	32	34	37	40
	WAIST	24	26	28	30	33
	HIP	33	34	37	40	43

SQUARE SCARF

A SQUARE SCARF IS A GREAT ENTRY-LEVEL PRINTING *and sewing project because it uses just a small piece of fabric and simple hems. Because you don't have to think about fit, and because you can hide printing errors when you fold your scarf, it gives you the freedom to play around with color and placement. In this example, I use a simple straight repeat pattern that is centered within the cut fabric panel, but I also include a decorative border and rotate my blocks as I print to provide more visual interest.*

Use a soft, lightweight fabric with a lot of drape for your scarves. I prefer to use either voile made of cotton or a cotton-silk blend or handkerchief linen. Just remember to use a needle intended for lightweight fabrics, or you risk snagging your fabric when you sew it.

MATERIALS AND TOOLS

Poppy and Poppy Border templates (page 155)

1 block cut to 4 × 4½ inches for the Poppy print

1 block cut to 1 × 4½ inches for the Poppy Border print

At least ½ cup of ink in 1 color

One 33-inch square panel of lightweight fabric (such as a cotton-silk blend, cotton voile, or handkerchief linen)

Matching thread

Quilting ruler

Sewing machine needle for lightweight fabrics

CARVE AND PRINT

1. Transfer the Poppy and Poppy Border images to your blocks, then carve and finish your blocks using the instructions in chapter 2.

2. Fold your fabric panel in half along the grainline, and press with your iron (see chapter 1 for how to find the grainline). Because you want your prints to be perfectly centered on your square scarf, fold your fabric in half again, this time perpendicular to the grainline, and press. Your fabric is now divided into four quadrants and has a clearly marked center.

3. Measure 4½ inches below the horizontal fold line and place the top of your quilting ruler there, aligning its vertical guides with the grainline (vertical) fold.

4. The repeat pattern for the main part of this scarf is a straight repeat with a horizontal offset of 4 inches and a vertical offset of 4½ inches. Mark your reference point anywhere along the bottom edge of your block.

5. Start by printing one impression in the center of your fabric below the horizontal fold as follows: Ink the Poppy block. Align the top of your block with the horizontal fold line (the bottom will rest on your quilting ruler), and place the center of your block on the vertical fold that marks your grainline. Make your first impression. Re-ink your block. Because the horizontal offset for this print is 4 inches, move the block 4 inches to the right, according to its reference point. Rotate the block 180 degrees to add visual interest (rotating the block is what makes this print "nondirectional"). Print your second impression, and continue printing to the right until you have made four impressions. Then print three impressions to the left of your first one for a total of seven impressions. Don't print to the edge of your fabric; you will leave this blank for now, and will later use your smaller block to create a border.

6. To create the next row, move your quilting ruler 4½ inches down (i.e., the vertical offset), and print this row the same way you printed the first. Continue in this manner until you have printed three rows below the horizontal fold line.

7. Next, rotate your fabric 180 degrees and print three more rows, following steps 4 through 6; you will have a total of six rows.

8. To create the border, place the top of your quilting ruler 1 inch from any of the edges of your fabric, aligning its vertical guides with the center fold line that intersects that edge. Ink the Poppy Border block. Place one of its short ends 1 inch to the right of the fold line, aligning the bottom of the block with the top of the ruler. Print. Re-ink your block. To make your second impression, move the reference point on your block 4½ inches to the right. Re-ink and make a third impression. Go back and print to the left of the center line in the same manner. Rotate your fabric and continue to print your border in this manner on the other three edges of your fabric panel.

9. Allow the ink on your fabric to dry, then heat-set it following the instructions in chapter 2.

SEW

10. Fold each of the edges ¼ inch toward the wrong side of the fabric. Fold the edges over again, another ¼ inch, and press well.

11. Topstitch the folded hems into place, using a ¼-inch seam allowance and your machine's needle for lightweight fabrics.

DESIGN IT YOURSELF!

- *TRY THIS AS A TWO-COLOR PRINT, USING DIFFERENT COLORS FOR THE BORDER AND CENTER PRINT.*

- *FOLLOW THE INSTRUCTIONS FOR PRINTING THE BORDER, BUT PRINT THE CENTER IMAGE FREE-FORM, AND USING A VARIETY OF BLOCKS.*

- *SKIP THE BORDER PRINT ALTOGETHER AND PRINT ALL THE WAY TO THE EDGE OF THE FABRIC.*

Tip THE HEMS ON SCARVES AVAILABLE IN STORES TEND TO BE ⅛ INCH. HOWEVER, THE SMALLEST HEM SIZE POSSIBLE USING THE PRESSER FOOT OF MOST HOME SEWING MACHINES IS ¼ INCH. IF YOU'D LIKE TO CREATE A SMALLER HEM, ⅛-INCH PRESSER FEET ARE AVAILABLE FOR MANY SEWING MACHINE MODELS. YOU CAN ALSO HAND SEW A ROLLED HEM USING COTTON OR SILK QUILTING THREAD. IT'S A TIME-CONSUMING PROCESS, BUT THE RESULT IS LOVELY.

OBLONG SCARF

WANT TO PRACTICE PRINTING A REPEAT PATTERN *without committing to sewing it into a fitted garment? Then this oblong scarf is the perfect project for you. Using just one block in two colors and the simplest of sewing stitches, this scarf can easily be made, start to finish, in a day.*

MATERIALS AND TOOLS

Dahlia template (page 153)

1 block cut to 6 inches square

2 (complementary) colors of ink, at least ½ cup of each

One 22 × 87-inch panel of lightweight fabric (such as a cotton-silk blend, cotton voile, or handkerchief linen)

Matching thread

Quilting ruler

Sewing machine needle for lightweight fabrics

CARVE AND PRINT

1. Transfer the Dahlia image to your block, then carve and finish it using the instructions in chapter 2. Trim your block so that it is approximately 5 inches in diameter.

2. This is a two-color print. The repeat pattern for each color is a straight repeat with 6-inch horizontal and vertical offsets. Mark the bottom center of your block as your reference point.

3. Fold the fabric panel in half lengthwise along the grainline, and press with your iron. Place the top of your quilting ruler 6½ inches from the top (i.e., one of the short ends) of your fabric, and align the 11-inch mark on the ruler with the grainline.

4. Ink your block with your first color. Place the inked block face down, with the reference point at the 5-inch mark on your ruler, and make your first impression. Re-ink your block and make your second impression 6 inches to the right. Since the reference point of your first impression is at the 5-inch mark, then the reference point of your second impression will be at the 11-inch mark, centered perfectly on the grainline that you've marked. The third impression will be at the 17-inch mark.

   I like the way this scarf looks with a hint of the image on its border, so I made a fourth impression at the 23-inch mark. This means that I needed to go back to the left edge and print there to balance the print. To do this, move your ruler over so that the 14-inch mark aligns with the grainline. The center of your original, first impression will now be at the 8-inch mark. Place your block's reference point at the 2-inch mark, and print.

5. To print the second row, move your quilting ruler down 6 inches, realign the 11-inch mark of your ruler with the grainline, and print, using the same measurements you did in the first row. Continue printing until you have filled your fabric. You should have 14 rows of the first color.

6. Wash your block and allow it to dry, and allow the ink on your scarf to dry to the touch before printing the second color.

7. To print the second color, measure 10 inches from the top, and again align the 11-inch mark on your ruler with the grainline you ironed in step 3.

8. Ink your block, align the reference point with the 8-inch mark on your ruler, and make your first impression. Re-ink your block, align the reference point with the 14-inch mark, and make your second impression. There are just two columns of the second color in this scarf, so move on to the next row.

9. To print the next row, move your quilting ruler down 6 inches and print, using the same measurements you did in the first row. Continue until you have printed all the rows.

10. Allow the ink on your scarf to dry completely, then heat set it following the instructions in chapter 2.

SEW

11. Fold the edges ¼ inch toward the wrong side of the fabric. Fold the edges again, another ¼ inch, and press well.

12. Topstitch the folded hems into place, using a ¼-inch seam allowance and your machine's needle for lightweight fabrics.

DESIGN IT YOURSELF!

- FIRST PRINT A BORDER ON THE SHORT ENDS OF THE SCARF USING A STRAIGHT REPEAT PATTERN, THEN PRINT FREE-FORM BETWEEN THE BORDERS. THIS ALSO LOOKS GREAT WHEN YOU USE THE SAME BLOCK FOR THE BORDERS AND THE BODY BUT DIFFERENT COLORS.

- DEPENDING ON HOW YOU WRAP YOUR SCARF, ONLY THE SHORT ENDS OF THE SCARF MAY SHOW WHEN YOU WEAR IT. IN THIS CASE, YOU CAN PRINT JUST THE ENDS OF THE SCARF. THIS IS ESPECIALLY HANDY WHEN YOU NEED TO MAKE A QUICK GIFT.

ESPADRILLES

THIS PROJECT REQUIRES JUST HALF A YARD OF FABRIC, *so it's a great way to use up your scraps. There is also very little machine sewing involved in this project. The bulk of the work is hand sewing the fabric to the sole. If you're looking for a fun vacation project, machine sew the fabric pieces together before you leave home, then hand stitch your espadrilles together on the plane, next to the pool, or while lying on the beach.*

MATERIALS AND TOOLS

Crocus and Dots templates
(page 152)

1 block cut to 3 × 4 inches for
the Crocus

1 block cut to 2 × 2½ inches for
the Dots

2 colors of ink, at least ½ cup
of each

½ yard of medium-weight fabric,
such as linen, for the exterior of
the espadrille

½ yard of plain, soft, medium-
weight fabric, such as chambray
or shirting fabric, for the lining

¼ yard of heavy fusible
interfacing or espadrille
stabilizer

Flat espadrille soles (available at
craft sores and online)

5 yards of espadrille thread

Upholstery needle

Thread wax

Pins

CARVE AND PRINT

1. Transfer the Crocus and Dots images to your blocks, then carve
   and finish your blocks using the instructions in chapter 2. Trim the
   Crocus block so it is approximately 3 × 2½ inches. Trim the Dots
   block so it is 2 × 1¾ inches.

2. Print your first color on the exterior fabric using the Dots block. This
   layer does not use a repeat pattern. Instead, make impressions
   randomly, rotating the block as you print. Allow the ink to become
   dry to the touch before printing the second color.

3. The repeat pattern for the second color is a half-drop repeat. The
   horizontal offset in each row is 3¼ inches, and the vertical offset in
   each column is 3½ inches. The vertical offset from the first regular
   column to the first half-drop column is 1¾ inches. (See chapter
   3 for detailed instructions on printing half-drop repeats.) Measure
   carefully and make your impressions until you have printed all your
   fabric.

4. Allow the ink to dry completely, then heat-set it following the
   instructions in chapter 2.

5. Your espadrille soles will come with cutting templates for the heel, toe, and interfacing. Use them to cut your fabric.

6. Iron the interfacing onto the wrong side of the printed fabric.

7. With right sides together, sew the exterior toe fabric to the lining fabric, using a ⅜-inch seam allowance. Leave a 2-inch gap unsewed on one side; you will use this to turn the fabric inside out later. Trim the seam allowance in half. Repeat for the other shoe.

8. Repeat step 7 with the exterior heel fabric, heel lining, and heel interfacing.

9. Turn the heels and toes right side out, through the gap you left on the sides. Push out the corners with a chopstick or knitting needle. Press well, then sew the gaps closed.

10. On the lined side of a toe piece, measure ⅝ inch from the bottom on both the right and left side. Align the edges of the short ends of a heel piece with this ⅝-inch mark on the toe, with the right side of the heel piece tucked behind the toe lining. Pin in place. Topstitch along the bottom edge of the toe from one side to the other, sewing the heel to the toe. Topstitch again ¼ inch away to strengthen the seam. Repeat for the other toe and heel pieces.

11. Pin the fabric to the sole: Fold the fabric in half to find the center of the toe and the center of the heel. Mark each with tailor's chalk or a pin. Pin the fabric to the sole, aligning the center of the toe and heel to the respective centers of the sole. Continue to pin your fabric to the sole at intervals of ¼ to ½ inch, aligning the edges of the fabric with the edges of the sole. You will need a lot of pins for this. You may have more fabric than sole; if this happens, redistribute fabric evenly among the pins along the front of the toe.

DESIGN IT YOURSELF!

- *USE DIFFERENT PRINTS FOR THE HEEL AND THE TOE. THIS IS MY FAVORITE WAY TO USE UP MY FABRIC SCRAPS.*

- *ADD DECORATIVE ACCENTS: EMBROIDERY, POM-POMS, OR BUTTONS.*

- *CUT OUT A BIT OF THE FRONT TOE AREA BEFORE SEWING THE TOE PIECES TOGETHER (REMEMBERING TO FACTOR IN A ⅜-INCH SEAM ALLOWANCE) TO MAKE A PEEP-TOE ESPADRILLE.*

- *SEW A LOOP ONTO THE BACK OF THE HEELS, AND RUN A YARD OF RIBBON THROUGH EACH LOOP TO MAKE A PRETTY ANKLE STRAP.*

- *IF YOU'D LIKE TO MAKE A DRESSIER SHOE, WEDGE-HEEL ESPADRILLE SOLES ARE ALSO AVAILABLE. THE SEWING INSTRUCTIONS FOR THESE ARE PRETTY MUCH THE SAME, THOUGH THEY REQUIRE LESS FABRIC.*

12. Cut 2½ yards of espadrille thread. You will use this one, long piece of thread to assemble the first espadrille. Pull the thread through the wax to coat it. The wax will keep your thread from snagging on the jute sole and make it easier to pull your thread through the sole and fabric. Thread your espadrille needle and knot the thread at the end.

13. Use a blanket stitch to attach the fabric to the sole: Start stitching from the side of the sole, close to where the toe and heel fabric are joined. Insert the needle into the sole, halfway between the top and bottom of the sole, and bring the needle up through the top of the sole and through your fabric about ¼ inch from the edge of the fabric. Pull your thread taut to embed the knot in the sole.

    Reinsert your needle ¼ inch from your first stitch on the side of the sole, and bring it back up through the sole and the fabric ¼ inch from the last stitch in the fabric, catching the loop of your first stitch with your needle, and pull it through. This is a blanket stitch. Continue in this manner, creating stitches about ¼ inch apart and keeping your stitches taut as you sew, until you have returned to where you started.

14. To finish your sole stitches, stitch through the final hole in the sole twice, and then stitch through your fabric three times in place. Knot the thread and clip the excess. Repeat steps 10 through 14 for the other espadrille.

CROSS-BODY BAG

TOO OFTEN, THE STRAPS ON CROSS-BODY BAGS *are too short or too long, and they can't be adjusted as needed. I designed the strap for this bag to be adjustable, so you can easily shorten or lengthen it on the go.*

MATERIALS AND TOOLS

California Spicebush template
(page 151)

1 block cut to 5 × 7 inches

½ cup of ink

1 yard of 60-inch-wide or
1½ yards of 44-inch-wide
medium-weight fabric (such as
linen or a linen-cotton blend),
for the bag's exterior

½ yard of 44-inch-wide (or
wider) medium-weight fabric
(muslin, twill, linen, or a linen-
cotton blend), for the unprinted
lining

PATTERN PIECES

G1	bag exterior: cut 2 from fabric	G3	long strap: cut 2 from fabric
G2	bag lining: cut 2 from lining	G4	short strap: cut 1 from fabric

FABRIC CUTTING GUIDE

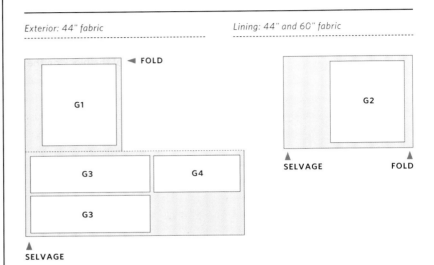

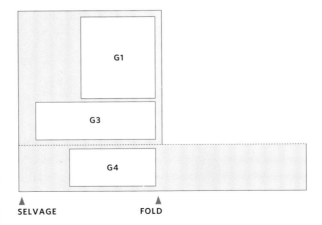

CARVE AND PRINT

1. Transfer the California Spicebush image to your block, then carve and finish it using the instructions in chapter 2. Trim your block around the image, leaving at least ⅛ inch between the edge of your image and the edge of your block. Your block will now measure approximately 5 × 6½ inches.

2. Print your exterior fabric, referring to the instructions in chapter 3. This print uses a half-drop repeat pattern, with a 180-degree rotation of the block on the half-drop. The horizontal offset is 4½ inches, and the vertical offset on each column is 7 inches. The vertical offset from the first regular column to the first half-drop column is 3½ inches. Measure out your offsets and make your impressions until you have printed all your fabric.

3. Allow the ink on your fabric to dry, and heat-set it following the instructions in chapter 2.

CUT AND SEW

4. Cut the pattern pieces from your fabric, transferring all the markings from the pattern to the fabric using tailor's chalk.

5. Line up the long strap pieces, right sides together, and sew along one short end. Press the seam allowance open.

6. Fold the long strap in half lengthwise with right sides together. Press well. Sew along the long edge and one short end. Turn the strap right side out, pushing your fabric through the short end that you left unsewn. Press. Repeat for the short strap.

7. Lay one piece of the exterior fabric flat, right side up. Place the unfinished end of the short strap on top of the outer fabric, aligning it with the marks on the fabric. Place the lining fabric on top of the outer fabric and strap, right sides together. Pin, and sew along the top edge of the bag, where the strap connects to the bag. Repeat with the long strap and your other panels of exterior and lining fabric.

8. Open up both sewn fabric panels and press the seam allowances toward the lining. Place the two sewn fabric panels right sides together, matching the fabric panels at the seams where the lining fabric and the exterior fabric meet. Pin in place, be sure to keep the loose ends of the straps tucked away from the edges. Sew around all four sides, leaving a 4-inch gap in the bottom of the lining.

9. Pull your fabric through the gap in the lining to turn the bag right side out. Sew the gap closed. Place the lining inside the bag.

10. Press the bag well, then edgestitch along the top of the bag.

11. Tie the straps together in a knot. You may need to adjust where you tie, based on your height and preferences.

DESIGN IT YOURSELF!

- *ADD AN EXTERIOR POCKET TO THE FRONT OF THE BAG.*

- *USE A DIFFERENT PRINT, OR THE SAME PRINT IN A DIFFERENT COLOR PALETTE, FOR THE STRAPS.*

- *INSTEAD OF USING PLAIN FABRIC FOR YOUR LINING, LINE YOUR BAG WITH ONE OF YOUR TEST PRINTS.*

TOTE BAG

THIS PATTERN IS BASED ON A BAG I USED TO SELL. *It's large enough to hold a laptop and a sketchbook, but not so large that it suggests you're heading to the beach. The leather straps, which are available at leather hobby stores, add a polished touch.*

MATERIALS AND TOOLS

Sticky Monkey Flower template
(page 157)

1 block cut to 4 × 6 inches

½ cup of ink

¾ yard of 44-inch-wide (or
wider) medium-weight fabric
(such as linen or a linen-cotton
blend), for the bag's exterior

¾ yard of 44-inch-wide (or
wider) medium-weight fabric
(cotton twill, or medium-weight
linen or a linen-cotton blend),
for the unprinted lining

¾ yard of fusible interfacing

Two leather straps, 1 × 25 inches
(or longer if you prefer)

Leather hole-punch tool

Eight ⅜-inch double-cap metal
rivets

Rivet-setting tool or hammer

PATTERN PIECES

F1	bag exterior: cut 2 from fabric, 2 from interfacing
F2	lining: cut 2 from lining
F3	pocket: cut 1 from lining
F4	strap template: transfer cutting marks to leather strap

FABRIC CUTTING GUIDE

Exterior: 44" and 60" fabric

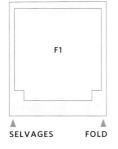

SELVAGES   FOLD

Lining: 60" fabric

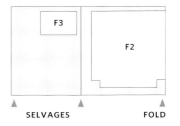

SELVAGES   FOLD

Lining: 44" fabric

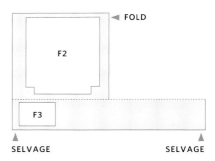

SELVAGE   SELVAGE

DESIGN IT YOURSELF!

- *MAKE FABRIC STRAPS INSTEAD OF USING LEATHER STRAPS. INSERT THE SEWN FABRIC STRAPS BETWEEN THE LINING AND THE EXTERIOR FABRIC IN STEP 8 AND SEW THEM IN.*

- *USE A DIFFERENT FABRIC FOR THE BOTTOM 8 INCHES OF THE BAG. CUT THE TWO EXTERIOR PANELS 8 INCHES SHORTER THAN THE PATTERN PIECE CALLS FOR, AND MAKE TWO NEW BOTTOM PIECES THAT ARE 9 INCHES HIGH. SEW EACH TOP TO ITS BOTTOM, THEN TREAT IT AS ONE PANEL (MEASUREMENTS ACCOUNT FOR SEAM ALLOWANCES).*

CARVE AND PRINT

1. Transfer the Sticky Monkey Flower image to your block, then carve and finish your block using the instructions in chapter 2. Do not trim your block.

2. Print your exterior fabric, referring to the instructions in chapter 3. This print uses a half-drop repeat pattern. The horizontal offset is 4 inches, and the vertical offset on each column is 6 inches. The vertical offset from the first regular column to the first half-drop column is 3 inches. Measure out your offsets and make your impressions until you have printed all your fabric.

3. Allow the ink on your fabric to dry, and heat-set it using the instructions in chapter 2.

4. Cut the pattern pieces from your fabric and interfacing, transferring all the markings from the pattern to the fabric using tailor's chalk.

5. Iron the fusible interfacing to the wrong side of your bag's exterior fabric pieces.

6. Fold the bottom and the right and left sides of the pocket to the wrong side of the fabric by ¼ inch. Press well.

7. Fold the top edge of the pocket ¼ inch toward the wrong side of the fabric, then fold another ¼ inch. Press, then topstitch ¼ inch from the top. Match the top corners of the pocket to the marks on the lining, and place the wrong side of the pocket against the right side of the lining. Pin in place and topstitch the sides and bottom.

8. Lay one of the printed exterior fabric panels on top of the lining, right sides together. Sew along the top edge. Repeat with the other lining and exterior fabric panels. Open up both sewn fabric panels and press the seam allowances open.

9. Place the two fabric panels on top of each other, right sides together, matching the fabric panels at the seams where the lining fabric and the exterior fabric meet. Pin together, then sew along all four sides of the bag, leaving a 4-inch gap in the bottom of the lining. Do not sew the square cutouts on the corners of the fabric—leave these open for now. These will serve as the gussets.

10. Pinch together the square cutouts on the corners of the fabric so the edges of the fabric align, and so the side and bottom seams align. Pin and sew.

11. Pull your bag right side out through the hole in the lining. You may need to push the corners out a bit with a turner or a chopstick. Sew the hole closed.

12. Place the lining inside the bag, so the printed exterior of the bag faces out. Press well. Topstitch around the top of the bag, 2 inches from the edge, to prevent the lining from moving around.

13. Attach the leather handles: Using your leather hole punch, punch small holes into your bag, as indicated by the dot marks you transferred from the pattern. Punch small holes into your leather straps at the dot marks. Align the holes in your leather straps with the holes in your bag. Insert the rivets, with the removable cap of the rivet on the inside of your bag. Place your rivet-setting tool on top of one of the rivet caps on the interior of the bag and set the rivet. Continue until you have set all 8 rivets.

APRON

A HALF-APRON IS ONE OF THE FIRST THINGS *I learned to sew. It's a simple, one-size-fits-all garment, made of just a few pieces of rectangular fabric. For my aprons, I like to use stronger, darker fabrics—such as the oatmeal linen used here. Aprons get a lot of wear and are meant to get dirty, so I prefer a durable fabric that will hold up well after multiple washings.*

MATERIALS AND TOOLS

Cameo Tulip template (page 152)

1 block cut to at least 3½ × 5¾ inches

½ cup of ink

1 yard of 44-inch-wide (or wider) medium-weight fabric (such as linen or a linen-cotton blend)

CARVE AND PRINT

1. Transfer the Cameo Tulip image to your block, then carve and finish your block using the instructions in chapter 2. Trim your block around the edge of your image, leaving a ¼-inch border between the edge of your image and the edge of your block.

2. Print your fabric, following the instructions in chapter 3. This print uses a half-drop repeat pattern. The horizontal offset is 3 inches, and the vertical offset on each column is 6 inches. The vertical offset from the first regular column to the first half-drop column is 3 inches. Measure out your offsets and make your impressions until you have printed all your fabric.

3. Allow the ink on your fabric to dry, and heat-set it using the instructions in chapter 2.

CUT AND SEW

4. Cut out the fabric as follows: one 28 x 22-inch panel for the body of your apron; one 16 × 13-inch panel for the pocket; and two 36 × 4-inch panels for the straps.

5. Fold all the sides of the pocket fabric ½ inch toward the wrong side, and press. Fold again to completely enclose the raw edges of your fabric, and press again. Pin the folds and topstitch all four sides ½ inch from the edge. Using a ruler and your tailor's chalk or a fabric marker, measure and draw a line down the middle of the pocket fabric, parallel to the short sides.

6. Fold the edges of the fabric for the body of the apron ½ inch toward the wrong side, along the short edges and the bottom long edge (these edges will be the two sides and the bottom of the apron). Press. Fold again ½ inch to completely enclose the raw edges of your fabric, and press again. Pin the folded hems place and topstitch along the top edge of the inner fold.

7. Align the center of the pocket with the center of the apron body. The pocket will be 6½ inches from either side of the apron and 5½ inches from its top and bottom. Pin it in place and topstitch along the sides and bottom. Next, stitch down the middle of the pocket, following the line you marked, to divide the pocket into two.

8. Place the apron straps right sides together. Sew along one of the short ends. Press the seam allowance open.

9. Fold the long strap in half lengthwise with wrong sides together. Press. Open the folded strap. Fold all four sides of the strap under by ½ inch toward the wrong side. Press.

10. Insert the unfinished top of the apron body into the folded strap, aligning the top of the apron with the center fold of the strap. Align the center of the apron with the center seam on the strap. Pin in place, and edgestitch along the sides and across the bottom of the strap.

DESIGN IT YOURSELF!

- *SEW EXTRA COLUMNS OF STITCHES ON THE POCKET TO CREATE COMPARTMENTS THAT CAN HOLD YOUR COOKING UTENSILS.*

- *ENLARGE OR SHRINK THE POCKET.*

- *LENGTHEN THE STRAP SO YOU CAN TIE THE APRON IN FRONT.*

- *MIX PRINTS: USE SCRAPS FROM OTHER PROJECTS TO CREATE THE POCKET.*

FOLDOVER CLUTCH

WHEN CHOOSING FABRIC FOR YOUR FOLDOVER CLUTCH, *select something that will wear well, because a clutch gets handled a lot. I prefer to use a darker, heavier fabric for the exterior and something much lighter weight for the lining. Too heavy of a lining may give the bag a bulky appearance and make it harder to fold.*

MATERIALS AND TOOLS

Anemones, Anemone Centers, and Anemone Leaf templates (page 150)

2 blocks cut to 5 × 5 inches for the anemones

2 blocks cut to 2 × 2 inches, one for each of the centers

1 block cut to 2½ × 3½ inches for the leaf

3 colors of ink, at least ¼ cup each

½ yard of 44-inch-wide (or wider) medium-weight fabric (such as linen or a linen-cotton blend), for the bag's exterior

½ yard of lightweight or medium-weight fabric for the unprinted lining

12-inch zipper

Zipper foot for your sewing machine

CARVE AND PRINT

1. Transfer the images to your blocks, then carve and finish your blocks using the instructions in chapter 2. Trim your blocks around the edge of the images, leaving a ¼-inch border between the edge of your images and the edge of your blocks.

2. Print your exterior fabric, referring to the instructions in chapter 3. This print does not use a repeat pattern. Rather, cluster the anemone impressions in groups of three, allowing them to overlap. Place the clusters randomly over the fabric. Let each color become dry to the touch before printing the next color.

3. Allow the ink on your fabric to dry, and heat-set it using the instructions in chapter 2.

CUT AND SEW

4. Cut out the fabric as follows: two 13 × 16-inch panels from your exterior fabric; two 13 × 15¾-inch panels from your lining fabric.

5. Fold one of the short edges of each of the exterior fabric panels under ½ inch toward the wrong side. Press.

6. Place the folded edge of each panel of exterior fabric, right side facing out, on top of the right side zipper tape, folded edges as close as possible to the zipper teeth. Pin in place, with the pins parallel to the fold. Using your machine's zipper foot, edgestitch ⅛ inch from the folded edge, removing pins as you go. You may also need to open and close the zipper to help you navigate the zipper foot as you sew.

7. Place the closed zipper and exterior fabric wrong side up. Align one of the short edges of the lining fabric with the edge of the zipper tape, with the right side of the lining against the wrong side of the zipper. Using your zipper foot and holding the exterior fabric out of the way, sew the lining to your zipper tape as close as possible to the fold. Repeat with the other piece of lining fabric.

- *FOR A FUN CONTRAST, INSTEAD OF USING TWO PANELS OF ONE PRINT FOR THE BAG'S EXTERIOR, USE FOUR PIECES OF FABRIC IN TWO DIFFERENT PRINTS. CUT TWO PIECES OF FABRIC THAT MEASURE 13 × 12 INCHES AND TWO PIECES OF FABRIC MEASURING 13 × 5 INCHES. SEW EACH OF THE LARGER PIECES TO ONE OF THE SMALLER PIECES ALONG THE LONGER SIDE OF EACH PIECE TO CREATE EACH EXTERIOR PANEL OF THE BAG, THEN CONTINUE TO SEW ACCORDING TO THE INSTRUCTIONS. THIS IS A GREAT WAY TO USE UP YOUR SCRAPS.*

- *USE SOME OF YOUR TEST FABRIC FOR THE LINING.*

- *ENLARGE YOUR BAG TO FIT THE DIMENSIONS OF YOUR LAPTOP, ADDING A LAYER OF THIN BATTING FOR PADDING.*

- *CREATING SMALLER BAGS IS SIMPLE. JUST BUY THE APPROPRIATE-SIZE ZIPPER AND ADJUST YOUR MEASUREMENTS ACCORDINGLY. BECAUSE WE ARE USING A ½-INCH SEAM ALLOWANCE, YOUR FABRIC SHOULD BE 1 INCH WIDER THAN THE LENGTH OF YOUR ZIPPER.*

8. Unzip the zipper halfway. Unfold your bag in such a way that the right sides of the exterior fabric panels are together, and the right sides of the lining are also together. Make sure to align the sides of the outer fabrics at the zipper first, with the zipper teeth folded toward the lining. Pin the exterior panels together along their perimeter, and do the same with the lining panels.

9. Using your sewing machine's regular foot, stitch along the edges of the sides and bottom of the exterior and then of the lining. Leave a 4-inch gap in the bottom of the lining so you will be able to turn your bag right side out. Clip the corners of the seams to reduce bulk.

10. Pull your bag right side out through the hole in the lining. You may need to push the corners out a bit with a turner or a chopstick.

11. Tuck in the raw edges of the gap in the lining and sew closed. Push the lining into the body of the bag. Press well.

CAP-SLEEVED BLOUSE

THIS BLOUSE PATTERN HAS NO FASTENINGS, *and it gets its shape from bust darts rather than from a fitted silhouette. It is a quick and easy sew, and a great project for beginners.*

MATERIALS AND TOOLS

Scandinavian Bloom and
Scandinavian Stem templates
(page 156)

1 block cut to 3½ × 4½ inches
for the bloom

1 block cut to 2½ × 3½ inches
for the stem

2 complementary colors of ink,
at least ½ cup of each

1½ yards of 44-inch or 60-inch
lightweight or medium-weight
woven fabric

¼ yard fusible interfacing

Thread

PATTERN PIECES

A1	front: cut 1 from fabric on fold
A2	back: cut 1 from fabric on fold
A3	front neck facing: cut 1 from fabric on fold; cut 1 from interfacing on fold
A4	back neck interfacing: cut 1 from fabric on fold; cut 1 from interfacing on fold
A5	arm binding: cut 2 from fabric

FABRIC CUTTING GUIDE

44" fabric

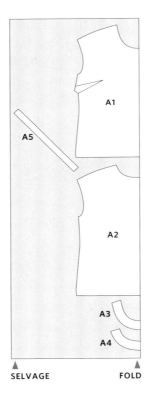

60" fabric

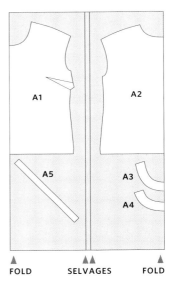

CARVE AND PRINT

1. Transfer the images to your blocks, then carve and finish your blocks using the instructions in chapter 2. Trim your blocks around the edge of the images, leaving a ⅛- to ¼-inch border between the edge of your images and the edge of your blocks.

2. Print your fabric, referring to the instructions in chapters 3 and 4 for a two-color print with precise registration. Print the stem first, following the measurements for a half-drop repeat pattern. The horizontal offset is 4 inches, and the vertical offset within a column is 6 inches. The vertical offset from the first column to the first half-drop column is 3 inches. You do not need to worry about the offset measurements of the flower block, as they were taken into account in the offset measurements of the stem block; all you have to do is line up the flowers with the stems.

3. Allow the ink on your fabric to dry, then heat-set it using the instructions in chapter 2.

CUT AND SEW

4. Cut the pattern pieces from your fabric and interfacing, transferring all the markings from the pattern to the fabric.

5. Fuse the interfacing to the wrong side of the neck facings following the manufacturer's instructions.

6. With the right sides together, sew the front neck facing to the back neck facing at the short ends. Press the seams open and trim the seam allowance to ¼ inch. Using a serger or a zigzag stitch, finish the bottom edges of the neck facing.

7. Sew the bust darts on the wrong side of the blouse front. Press the darts down, toward the side seams. Place the blouse front on top of the blouse back with right sides together, and align at the shoulders. Sew along the shoulders. Using a serger or zigzag stitch, finish the seam allowances together and press them toward the back of the blouse.

DESIGN IT YOURSELF!

■ *USE A DIFFERENT FABRIC—*
EITHER PLAIN FABRIC OR
LEFTOVER PRINTED FABRIC
FROM ANOTHER PROJECT—
FOR THE NECK FACING AND
ARMHOLE BINDING.

8. Pin the right side of the neck facing to the right side of the blouse, aligning the raw edges of the neckline; align the facing's side seams with the shoulders of the blouse, and its top center with the top center of the front neckline. Sew the facing to the neckline using a ¼-inch seam allowance. Clip the seam allowance perpendicular to your stitches, being careful not to cut your stitches. This will help the rounded areas to lie flat.

9. Press the seam allowance and the neck facing up and away from the blouse, then understitch the neckline by sewing the facing to the seam allowance ⅛ inch from the seam. Trim the seam allowance to just a little over ⅛ inch. Turn the facing to the inside of the neckline and press well. Pin the facing in place and press well, until the facing lies flat. Topstitch close to the bottom edge of the neck facing. Press well.

10. With the right sides together, sew the side seams of the blouse from the bottom of the armhole to the bottom of the blouse. Using a serger or zigzag stitch, finish the seam allowances together and press them toward the back of the blouse.

11. Fold one arm binding in half with the right sides together, lining up the short edges. Sew the short edges together using a ⅜-inch seam allowance. Trim the seam allowance to ¼ inch, and press the seam open.

12. Placing right sides together, pin the binding to the armhole, aligning one of the raw edges of the binding with the raw edge of the armhole. Make sure to place the seam of the arm binding off to the side of the bottom seam of the armhole to prevent bulk. Pin in place and sew the binding to the armhole. Trim the seam allowance to ⅛ inch.

13. Fold the binding in half, then fold in half again to encase the raw edge. Turn the binding to the inside of the armhole and press well. Pin the binding in place, and topstitch ¼ inch from the edge of the armhole. Press well. Repeat steps 11 through 13 for the other armhole.

14. Fold the bottom hem under ⅜ inch toward the wrong side of the blouse. Press. Fold the hem under another ¾ inch and press again. Topstitch the hem by sewing to the top of the inside fold.

SHORT-SLEEVED BLOUSE

THIS IS ONE OF THE MOST VERSATILE GARMENTS I OWN. *I have made it in unprinted fabric to coordinate with my printed skirts, as well as in my hand-printed fabric. This pattern uses flat sleeves rather than set-in sleeves, making it another project suitable for beginners.*

MATERIALS AND TOOLS

Seed Pods template (page 157)

1 block cut to 3 × 4½ inches

2 complementary colors of ink, at least ½ cup of each

1¾ yards of 44-inch-wide OR 1¼ yards of 60-inch-wide lightweight or medium-weight woven fabric, for all sizes

¼ yard fusible interfacing

PATTERN PIECES

B1	front: cut 1 from fabric, on fold
B2	back: cut 1 from fabric, on fold
B3	sleeves: cut 2 from fabric
B4	front neck facing: cut 1 from fabric on fold; cut 1 from interfacing on fold
B5	back neck facing: cut 1 from fabric on fold; cut 1 from interfacing on fold

FABRIC CUTTING GUIDE

44" fabric

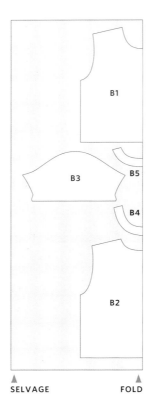

60" fabric

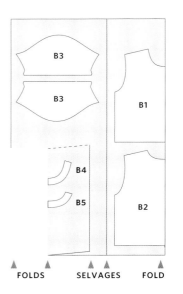

CARVE AND PRINT

1. Transfer the image to your block, then carve and finish your block using the instructions in chapter 2. Trim your block around the edge of the image, leaving a ⅛- to ¼-inch border between the edge of your image and the edge of your block.

2. Although the block is a simple design, this is a complex print: it uses a half-drop repeat pattern, a rotated block on the half-drop, and a second color every third impression. Before printing, write notes detailing your measurements and colors, and use them as a guide as you print.

3. Print your fabric, referring to the instructions in chapters 3 and 4. The horizontal offset is 2½ inches, and the vertical offset within a column is 5 inches. The vertical offset from the first column to the first half-drop column is 2½ inches. Allow the ink on your fabric to dry, and heat-set it using the instructions in chapter 2.

CUT AND SEW

4. Cut the pattern pieces from your fabric and interfacing, transferring all the markings from the pattern to the fabric.

5. Fuse the interfacing to the wrong side of the neck facings following the manufacturer's instructions.

6. With the right sides together, sew the front neck facing to the back neck facing at the short ends. Press the seams open. Using a serger or zigzag stitch, finish the bottom edges of the neck facing.

7. Place the blouse front on top of the blouse back, right sides together. Sew along the shoulders. Using a serger or zigzag stitch, finish the seam allowances together and press them toward the back of the blouse.

8. Pin the right side of the neck facing to the right side of the blouse, aligning the raw edges of the neckline; align the facing's side seams with the shoulders of the blouse, and its top center with the top

- *ADD A SMALL PATCH POCKET IN A CONTRASTING FABRIC.*

- *THE PRINT FOR THIS BLOUSE IS QUITE COMPLEX, WITH ITS A HALF-DROP REPEAT AND A SECOND COLOR FOR EVERY THIRD COLUMN. SIMPLIFY IT BY USING JUST ONE COLOR OR BY ALTERNATING THE COLORS EVERY OTHER COLUMN.*

center of the front neckline. Sew the facing to the neckline using a ¼-inch seam allowance. Clip the seam allowance perpendicular to your stitches, being careful not to cut your stitches. This will help the rounded areas to lie flat.

9. Press the seam allowance and the neck facing up and away from the blouse, then understitch the neckline by sewing the facing to the seam allowance ⅛ inch from the seam. Trim the seam allowance to just a little over ⅛ inch. Turn the facing to the inside of the neckline and press well. Pin the facing in place and press well, until the facing lies flat. Topstitch close to the bottom edge of the neck facing. Press well.

10. Attach the sleeves: Open the blouse and lay it flat, with its right side facing up. Align the midpoint marking on one sleeve to a shoulder seam, right sides together, and pin. Match the marks on the front and back of the sleeve with the corresponding marks on the front and back of the blouse. Pin in place. You may have extra fabric between the markings on the sleeve cap. If so, distribute the excess fabric evenly among the pins. Sew the sleeve to the blouse. Finish the seam allowances together and press them down, toward the sleeve. Repeat for the other sleeve.

11. Turn the blouse inside out, with right sides together. Match up the sleeve seams at the armpit and pin them together. Align and pin the side seams of the body. Starting at the cuff and working along the underarm then down toward the blouse's hem, sew the front and back of the blouse together. Repeat for the other side. Using a serger or zigzag stitch, finish your seam allowances together, and press them toward the back of the blouse.

12. Hem the sleeves: Fold the sleeve hem under ½ inch toward the wrong side and press. Fold the sleeve under another 1 inch, and press again. Topstitch the sleeve's hem by sewing close to the inside fold. Repeat for the other sleeve.

13. Hem the blouse: Fold the bottom hem up ½ inch toward the wrong side and press. Fold the hem up another 1 inch and press again. Topstitch the hem, sewing close to the inside fold.

COAT

FOR A LONG TIME I WAS INTIMIDATED BY THE IDEA *of sewing a coat, until I realized that an unlined, open coat is no more difficult to sew than a blouse or a skirt. With its flat sleeves and lack of fastenings, it's another great beginner garment. However, this coat does require a lot of fabric. I recommend using a nondirectional print, such as the William Morris Flower print used here, so you can maximize your yardage.*

MATERIALS AND TOOLS

William Morris Flower template
(page 159)

1 block cut to 5½ × 7 inches

At least ½ cup of ink

2⅝ yards of 44-inch OR
2 yards of 60-inch medium-
weight, woven fabric

1 yard fusible interfacing

PATTERN PIECES

F1	front: cut 2 from fabric
F2	back: cut 1 from fabric on fold
F3	front facing: cut 2 from interfacing
F4	sleeves: cut 2 from fabric
F5	back facing: cut 1 from fabric; cut 1 from interfacing
F6	pocket: cut 2 from fabric

FABRIC CUTTING GUIDE

44" fabric

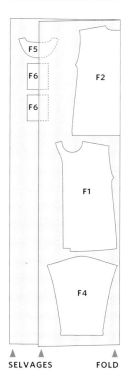

SELVAGES   FOLD

60" fabric

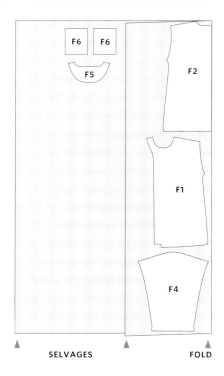

SELVAGES   FOLD

CARVE AND PRINT

1. Transfer the image to your block, then carve and finish your block using the instructions in chapter 2. Trim your block around the edge of the image, leaving approximately a ¼-inch border between the edge of your image and the edge of your block. Your finished block should measure about 5 × 6½ inches.

2. Print your fabric, referring to the instructions in chapter 3. This is a half-drop repeat pattern, with the block rotated 180 degrees on the half-drop. The horizontal offset is 4½ inches, and the vertical offset within a column is 6½ inches. The vertical offset from the first column to the first half-drop column is 3½ inches.

3. Allow the ink on your fabric to dry, then heat-set it using the instructions in chapter 2.

CUT AND SEW

4. Cut the pattern pieces from your fabric and interfacing, transferring all the markings from the pattern to the fabric.

5. Fuse the interfacing to the wrong side of the back facing and to the wrong side of the coat fronts following the manufacturer's instructions.

STEP
5

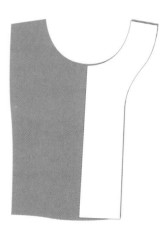

6. Align the coat fronts with the coat back, right sides together. Sew along the shoulders. Using a serger or zigzag stitch, finish the seam allowances together and press them toward the back.

7. Align the short ends of the back facing with the short ends of the interfaced coat fronts, with right sides together. Pin together and sew. Using a serger or zigzag stitch, finish the seam allowances together and press both toward the back facing.

STEP 7

8. Fold the coat front, right sides together, along the edge of the facing. Pin the facing along the neckline and back, matching the coat's shoulder seams with the seams where the coat front facings meet the back facing. Sew using a ¼-inch seam allowance. Using a serger or zigzag stitch, finish the unenclosed edges of the facings, starting from the bottom front of the right-hand side of the coat, up to and around

STEP 8

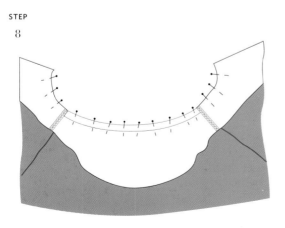

the neck facings, and then to the bottom of the left-hand side of the coat front.

9. Press the seam allowance and facing up and away from the coat body. Starting and ending 1 inch from the front folds, understitch the neckline by sewing the facing to the seam allowance ⅛ inch from the seam. Trim the seam allowance to just a little over ⅛ inch. Clip the seam allowance perpendicular to your stitches, being careful not to cut your stitches. This will help the rounded areas to lie flat.

10. Attach the sleeves: Open the coat and lay it flat, right side up. Align the midpoint marking on one sleeve to a shoulder seam, right sides together, and pin. Match the marks on the front and back of the sleeve with the corresponding marks on the front and back of the coat, and pin. You may have excess fabric between the markings on the sleeve cap. If so, distribute the excess fabric evenly among the pins. Sew the sleeve to the coat. Using a serger or zigzag stitch, finish the seam allowances together and press up toward the neckline. Topstitch ½ inch from the seam so the seam allowance will lie flat. Repeat for the other sleeve.

11. Turn the coat inside out, right sides facing in. Match up the sleeve seams at the armpit and pin them together. Align and pin the side seams along the body. Starting at the cuff, work along the arm, pivoting at the armpit, and working toward the coat's hem, to sew the front and back of the coat together. Repeat for the other side. Using a serger or zigzag stitch, finish your seam allowances together and press them toward the back of the coat. Turn the coat right side out.

12. Attach the pockets: Fold all four sides of one of your pockets ⅜ inch toward the wrong side and press. Fold the top another 1 inch, and press again. Topstitch along the inside fold. Repeat for the other pocket. Fold the sides and bottom of each pocket ½ inch toward the wrong side and press well. Align the top right and left corners of your pocket with the marks on the coat and pin in place. Topstitch the sides and bottom of your pocket. Repeat for the other pocket.

13. Fold a sleeve hem under ¼ inch toward the wrong side and press. Fold the hem under another 1 inch, and press again. Topstitch the sleeve's hem by sewing close to the inside fold. Repeat for the other sleeve.

14. Fold the coat hem under ¾ inch toward the wrong side and press. Fold the hem under another 1 inch, and press again. Sew the hem, sewing close to the inside fold.

15. Press the front facing of the coat well. Beginning 1 inch from the bottom front of one side of the coat, topstitch 1 inch from the edge of the coat's front opening. Continue to topstitch up the front of the coat, around the neckline, and down the other side of the coat front until you reach the bottom of other side of the coat front.

DESIGN IT YOURSELF!

- *USE CONTRASTING FABRIC FOR THE POCKETS, OR PRINT A SMALL AMOUNT OF THE FABRIC FOR THE POCKETS USING THE SAME BLOCK, ONLY IN A DIFFERENT, COMPLEMENTARY COLOR.*

- *SHORTEN THE COAT TO MAKE IT WAIST- OR HIP-LENGTH. IN THIS CASE, YOU'LL NEED TO PRINT LESS FABRIC.*

FULL SKIRT

FOR THE LONGEST TIME, I AVOIDED SEWING GARMENTS *that had invisible zippers because I found them so intimidating. I searched for patterns for wrap skirts and skirts with elastic waistbands, rather than plunge in and just learn how to sew an invisible zipper. Once I learned, though, I couldn't believe how silly I'd been to avoid them, and a whole new world of garments was opened to me. If you've never sewn an invisible zipper before, why not take the plunge and learn how with this skirt pattern? This is a beginner pattern.*

MATERIALS AND TOOLS

Olive Branch template
(page 156)

1 block cut to 2 × 6¼ inches

At least ½ cup of ink

2 yards of 44-inch OR 1⅔ yards
of 60-inch lightweight or
medium-weight woven fabric

¼ yard of fusible interfacing

8-inch invisible zipper

Invisible zipper foot for your
sewing machine

PATTERN PIECES

C1	front: cut 1 from fabric on fold
C2	back: cut 2 from fabric
C3	waistband: cut 1 from fabric
C4	pocket: cut 4 from fabric
C5	waistband interfacing: cut 1 from interfacing

FABRIC CUTTING GUIDE

44" fabric

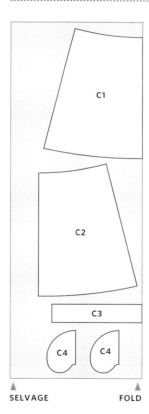

SELVAGE   FOLD

60" fabric

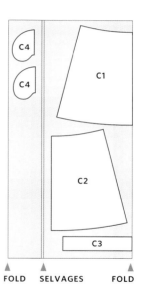

FOLD   SELVAGES   FOLD

1. Transfer the image to your block, then carve and finish your block using the instructions in chapter 2. Trim your block around the edge of the image, leaving a ¼-inch border between the edge of your image and the edge of your block.

2. Print your fabric, referring to the instructions in chapter 3. This is a half-drop repeat pattern, and the block is rotated 180 degrees on the half-drop. The horizontal offset is 2 inches, and the vertical offset within a column is 7 inches. The vertical offset from the first column to the first half-drop column is 3½ inches.

3. Allow the ink on your fabric to dry completely, and heat-set it using the instructions in chapter 2.

CUT AND SEW

DESIGN IT YOURSELF!

- *OMIT THE IN-SEAM POCKETS, AND SEW PATCH POCKETS ONTO THE FRONT OF THE SKIRT INSTEAD.*

- *USE A CONTRASTING PRINT FOR THE BOTTOM OF THE SKIRT. TO TRACE PATTERN PIECES FOR THE BORDER, TRACE THE BOTTOM 7 INCHES FROM THE BOTTOM OF THE SKIRT PATTERN PIECES, THEN ADD ½ INCH TO THE TOP FOR THE SEAM ALLOWANCE.*

4. Cut the pattern pieces from your fabric and interfacing, transferring all the markings from the pattern to the fabric.

5. Using a serger or zigzag stitch, finish each of the pocket pieces along their rounded edges, leaving only the straight edges unfinished. Place one front pocket piece on the skirt front, right sides together, matching the markings on the straight edge of the pocket with the markings on one side of the skirt front. Sew the pocket piece to the skirt front. Using a serger or zigzag stitch, finish the side seam allowance on that side of the skirt front, and press the pocket away from the skirt front. Repeat for the other front pocket piece and side seam allowance. Repeat the process for the back pocket pieces, again matching the markings on the pocket with the markings on the skirt and finishing the side seams.

6. With right sides together, align one side of the front skirt piece with the side of one of the skirt back panels, lining up the pockets. Starting at the top of the skirt on one side, sew the side seam, stopping ½ inch past the top edge of the pocket piece. Pivot, then sew the front pocket to the back pocket, pivoting again ½ inch into the skirt's seam allowance. Sew to the bottom of the skirt. Repeat for

the other skirt back panel. Press pockets and seam allowances toward the front.

7. Sew two rows of basting stitches along the top of the skirt, ¼ inch and ⅜ inch from the top edge, leaving at least two inches of thread on both sides. Do not backstitch at the beginning or end. Create gathers by gently pulling on the threads at both ends.

8. Fuse the interfacing to the bottom half of the waistband, following the manufacturer's instructions. Align the short ends of the waistband with the raw edges of the back panels, align the side notches on the waistband with the side seams of the skirt, and align the center notch on the waistband with the center notch of the skirt front. Pin, distributing the gathers evenly between the pins. Sew the waistband to the skirt.

9. Fold the unsewn long end of the waistband ½ inch toward the wrong side, and press well. Fold the waistband in half lengthwise with wrong sides together, and press well. Pin the folded edge to the wrong side of the skirt, making sure that it covers the stitches where the front of the waistband was sewn to the front of the skirt. Edgestitch in place.

10. Before inserting the invisible zipper, finish the edges of the back of the skirt, including the waistband, using a serger or zigzag stitch.

11. Open your zipper fully. On the wrong side of your zipper tape, use an iron set to low (too hot of an iron will melt your zipper tape) to press the zipper teeth away from the zipper tape, so that your zipper teeth are at a 90-degree angle from the zipper tape. Do not press your zipper teeth flat!

12. Place the left-hand side of the invisible zipper tape on the left-hand side of the skirt, right sides together. Align the side edge of your zipper tape with the edge of your fabric, and the top stopper with the top of your waistband. Pin in place. Using your invisible zipper foot, sew the zipper to the skirt, sewing just to the right of the zipper teeth. Be careful not to sew on the zipper teeth! Press the fabric back.

13. Turn the skirt inside out. Fold your zipper so that the right-hand side of the invisible zipper is now lying on the right-hand side of the skirt, right sides together. Pin in place. Again, using your invisible zipper foot, sew the zipper to the skirt, this time sewing to the left of the zipper teeth. Press the fabric back.

14. Close the zipper. Switch to your regular zipper foot, and sew the seam from the bottom of the zipper to the bottom of the skirt.

15. Beginning from the top of the waistband and ending at its bottom, topstitch the zipper and waistband together using a ¼-inch seam allowance.

16. Hem the skirt: Fold the skirt hem under ¼ inch toward the wrong side and press. Fold the hem under another 1 inch, and press again. Topstitch the hem, sewing close to the inside fold.

CAP-SLEEVED DRESS

THE SLIGHT CAP SLEEVE OF THIS DRESS IS A CHIC UPDATE *to the standard sleeveless dress, and keeps it from looking too season-specific. Sew it in a darker fabric in the fall and winter, and pair it with a cardigan or the coat.*

MATERIALS AND TOOLS

Fern Left and Fern Right templates (page 154)

2 blocks, each cut to 4 × 7 inches

2 (complementary) colors of ink, at least ½ cup of each

2⅓ yards of 44-inch or 60-inch lightweight or medium-weight woven fabric

14-inch invisible zipper

Invisible zipper foot for your sewing machine

PATTERN PIECES

D1	front: cut 1 from fabric on fold
D2	back: cut 2 from fabric
D3	front neck facing: cut 1 from fabric on fold; cut 1 from interfacing on fold
D4	back neck facing: cut 2 from fabric; cut 2 from interfacing
D5	arm binding: cut 2 from fabric
D6	pocket: cut 4 from fabric

FABRIC CUTTING GUIDE

44" fabric

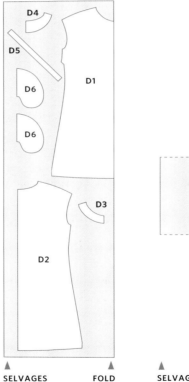

60" fabric

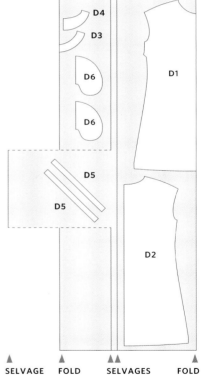

1. Transfer the images to your blocks, then carve and finish your blocks using the instructions in chapter 2. Trim your blocks around the edge of the images, leaving at least a ⅛-inch border between the edge of your images and the edge of your blocks.

2. Print your fabric, referring to the instructions in chapters 3 and 4. This is a two-color, straight repeat pattern. Start by printing the first color using the Fern Right block. The horizontal offset of the first color is 6½ inches, and the vertical offset is 7½ inches. Allow the first color to become dry to the touch before printing the second color.

3. Print the second color using the Fern Left block. Using a permanent marker, draw a straight line from the bottom of the stem on the front of the block, across the bottom side of the block, and to the back of the block. This will be your reference point for printing the second image. The bottom of the stem in this second color should be printed 2 inches directly above the bottom of the stem of the impressions you made in the first color. Place your quilting ruler so that the long end of the ruler aligns with the bottom of the first impression, then move your ruler 2 inches up. Make your first impression, and continue printing using a straight repeat pattern. The horizontal offset is 6½ inches, and the vertical offset is 7½ inches.

4. Allow the ink on your fabric to dry, then heat-set it using the instructions in chapter 2.

CUT AND SEW

5. Cut the pattern pieces from your fabric and interfacing, transferring all the markings from the pattern to the fabric.

6. Sew the bust darts on the wrong side of the dress front. Press the darts down, toward the hem.

7. Place the dress front panel on top of the dress back panels with right sides together and align the shoulder seams. Sew along the shoulders. Using a serger or zigzag stitch, finish the seam allowances together and press them toward the back.

8. Using a serger or zigzag stitch, finish each of the pocket pieces along their rounded edges, leaving the straight edges unfinished. Place one front pocket piece on the dress front, right sides together, matching the markings on the straight edge of the pocket with the markings on the side of the dress panel. Sew the pocket piece to the dress front. Repeat for the other front pocket piece. Repeat the process for the back pocket pieces, again matching the straight side on the pocket with the notches on the side of the dress. Finish the sides of the dress front and backs and press the pockets back, away from the dress panels.

9. With right sides together, align one side of the dress front panel with the side of one of the dress back panels, matching the bottoms of the armholes and the pocket pieces. Pin. Starting from the bottom of the armhole, sew the side seam, stopping ½ inch past the top edge of the pocket piece. Pivot, then sew the front pocket to the back pocket, pivoting again ½ inch into the dress's seam allowance. Continue to sew to the bottom hem of the dress. Repeat on the other side. Press pockets and seam allowances toward the front.

10. Open your zipper fully. On the wrong side of your zipper tape, use an iron set to low (too hot of an iron will melt your zipper tape) to press the zipper teeth away from the zipper tape, so that your zipper teeth are at a 90-degree angle from the zipper tape. Do not press your zipper teeth flat!

11. Turn your dress right side out. Place the left-hand side of the invisible zipper tape face down on the left-hand side of the dress, right sides together. Place the top zipper stopper ¼ inch from the top of the dress, and the side edge of your zipper tape ⅛ inch from the edge of your fabric. Pin in place. Using your invisible zipper foot, sew the zipper to the dress, sewing just to the right of the zipper teeth. Be careful not to sew on the zipper teeth! Press the fabric back.

12. Turn your dress inside out. Fold your zipper so that the right-hand side of the invisible zipper is now lying on the right-hand side of the dress, right sides together. Pin in place. Again, using your invisible zipper foot, sew the zipper to the dress, this time sewing to the left of the zipper teeth. Press the fabric back.

13. Close the zipper. Switch to your regular zipper foot, and sew the seam from the bottom of the zipper to the bottom of the dress.

14. Fold one arm binding in half with the right sides together, lining up the short edges. Sew the short edges together. Trim the seam allowance to ¼ inch, and press the seam open.

15. Turn the dress right side out. Placing right sides together, pin the binding to the armhole, aligning one of the raw edges of the binding with the raw edge of the armhole. Make sure to place the seam of the binding off to the side of the bottom seam of the armhole to prevent bulk. Pin in place, and sew the binding to the armhole using a ⅜-inch seam allowance. Trim the seam allowance to ⅛ inch.

16. Fold the binding in half, then fold in half again to encase the raw edge. Turn the binding to the inside of the armhole and press well. Pin the binding in place, and topstitch. Press well. Repeat steps 14 through 16 for the other armhole.

17. Fuse the interfacing to the wrong side of the neck facings following the manufacturer's instructions.

18. With right sides together, match the side seams of the front neck facing and the back neck facings and pin. Sew the side seams. Using a serger or zigzag stitch, finish the seam allowances together and press toward the back. Finish the bottom and side edges of the facing.

19. Pin the right side of the neck facing to the right side of the dress, raw edges together, with the facing's short ends aligned to the unsewn edges of the back panels, and with its seams aligned with the shoulder seams of the dress. The facing will cover the top part of your zipper tape. Starting from the bottom of one short edge of the facing, sew toward the neckline using a ¼-inch seam allowance. Stop ¼-inch from the neckline, pivot, then sew the facing to the neckline, again using a ¼-inch seam allowance. Stop when you are ¼ inch from the seam allowance on the other side, and again pivot, sewing just to the bottom of the neck facing.

STEP
19

- *SEW BELT LOOPS ONTO THE SIDES, AND ADD A SASH USING THE SAME OR COMPLEMENTARY FABRIC.*

- *OMIT THE IN-SEAM POCKETS, AND SEW PATCH POCKETS ONTO THE FRONT OF THE DRESS.*

20. Press the seam allowance and the neck facing up and away from the dress. Starting 1 inch from the zipper, understitch the neckline by sewing the facing to the seam allowance very close to the seam. Stop understitching 1 inch from the neckline on the other side. Trim the seam allowance to just a little over $\frac{1}{8}$ inch. Clip the seam allowance perpendicular to your stitches, careful not to cut your stitches. This will help the rounded areas to lie flat. Turn the facing to the inside of the neckline and press well. Pin the facing in place and press well, until the facing lies flat.

21. Beginning on one back panel, topstitch along the neckline $\frac{1}{4}$ inch from the edge.

22. Hem the dress: Fold the dress hem under $\frac{1}{4}$ inch toward the wrong side of the dress and press. Fold the hem under another 1 inch, and press again. Topstitch the hem by sewing close to the inside fold.

SHORT-SLEEVED DRESS

SEVEN YEARS AGO I BOUGHT ONE OF *my favorite dresses—a striped T-shirt dress—at a secondhand store, then wore it until it became too thin to be decent. For years, I looked for a woven version to replace it, until I figured out that I could ask Barrie and Kenny to design one for me. The result is this simple dress with flat sleeves and in-seam pockets. Made with hand-printed woven fabric, it's a sophisticated—yet incredibly comfortable—update of my favorite dress. This is an advanced beginner pattern.*

MATERIALS AND TOOLS

Turkish Tulip template
(page 158)

1 block cut to 6 × 7¾ inches

At least ½ cup of ink

2½ yards of 44-inch OR 1⅔
yards of 60-inch lightweight or
medium-weight woven fabric

¼ yard of fusible interfacing

13-inch invisible zipper

Invisible zipper foot for your
sewing machine

PATTERN PIECES

E1	front: cut 1 from fabric on fold
E2	back: cut 2 from fabric
E3	sleeves: cut 2 from fabric
E4	front neck facing: cut 1 from fabric on fold; cut 1 from interfacing on fold
E5	back neck facing: cut 2 from fabric; cut 2 from interfacing
E6	pocket: cut 4 from fabric

FABRIC CUTTING GUIDE

44" fabric

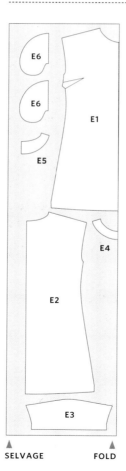

SELVAGE   FOLD

60" fabric

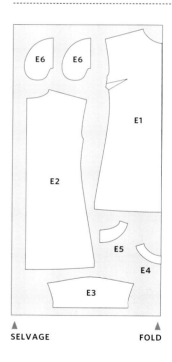

SELVAGE   FOLD

CARVE AND PRINT

1. Transfer the image to your block, then carve and finish your block using the instructions in chapter 2. Trim your block around the edge of the image, leaving at least a ¼-inch border between the edge of your image and the edge of your block.

2. Print your fabric, referring to the instructions in chapter 3. This is a bricked repeat pattern. The horizontal offset is 7 inches, and the vertical offset is 6½ inches. The horizontal offset from the first row to the first bricked row is 3½ inches.

3. Allow the ink on your fabric to dry, then heat set it using the instructions in chapter 2.

CUT AND SEW

4. Cut the pattern pieces from your fabric and interfacing, transferring all the markings from the pattern to the fabric.

5. Sew the bust darts on the wrong side of the dress front. Press the darts down, toward the hem.

6. Place the dress front panel on top of the dress back panels with right sides together and align at the shoulders. Sew along the shoulders. Using a serger or zigzag stitch, finish the seam allowances together and press them toward the back.

7. Using a serger or zigzag stitch, finish each of the pocket pieces along their rounded edges, leaving the straight edges unfinished. Place one front pocket piece on the dress front, right sides together, matching the markings on the straight side of the pocket with the markings on the side of the dress. Sew the pocket piece to the dress front. Repeat for the other front pocket piece. Repeat the process for the back pocket pieces, again matching the straight side on the pocket with the notches on the side of the dress. Finish the sides of the dress front and backs and press the pockets away from the dress.

8. Using a serger or zigzag stitch, finish the short sides of both sleeves.

9. Attach the sleeves: Open the dress and lay it flat, right side up. Align the midpoint marking on one sleeve to a shoulder seam, right sides together, and pin. Match the marks on the front and back of the sleeve with the corresponding marks on the front and back of the dress and pin. You may have excess fabric between the markings on the sleeve cap. If so, distribute the excess fabric evenly among the pins. Sew the sleeve to the dress. Using a serger or zigzag stitch, finish the seam allowances together and press them down, toward the sleeve. Repeat for the other sleeve.

10. Turn the dress wrong side out, with right sides together. Align one side of the dress front panel with the side of one of the dress back panels, matching the sleeves, the bottoms of the armholes, and the pocket pieces. Pin. Starting from the cuff of the sleeve, sew toward the armpit, stopping when your needle reaches the seam that connects the sleeve to the armhole. Pivot, then sew the side seam ½ inch past the top edge of the pocket piece, and backstitch there. Start sewing again ½ inch before the bottom of the pocket, and sew to the bottom hem of the dress. Then sew the pockets together. Repeat on the other side. Press pockets and seam allowances toward the front.

11. Open your zipper fully. On the wrong side of your zipper tape, use an iron set to low (too hot of an iron will melt your zipper tape) to press the zipper teeth away from the zipper tape, so that your zipper teeth are at a 90-degree angle from the zipper tape. Do not press your zipper teeth flat!

12. Turn your dress right side out. Place the left-hand side of the invisible zipper tape face down on the left-hand side of the dress, right sides together. Place the top zipper stopper ¼ inch from the top of the dress, and the side edge of your zipper tape ⅛ inch from the edge of your fabric. Pin in place. Using your invisible zipper foot, sew the zipper to the dress, sewing just to the right of the zipper teeth. Be careful not to sew on the zipper teeth! Press the fabric back.

13. Turn your dress inside out. Fold your zipper so that the right-hand side of the invisible zipper is now lying on the right-hand side of the dress, right sides together. Pin in place. Again, use your invisible zipper foot, sew the zipper to the dress, this time sewing to the left of the zipper teeth. Press the fabric back.

14. Close the zipper. Switch to your regular zipper foot, and sew the seam from the bottom of the zipper to the bottom of the dress.

15. Fuse the interfacing to the wrong side of the neck facings following the manufacturer's instructions.

16. With right sides together, align the side seams of the front neck facing and the back neck facings and pin. Sew the side seams. Using a serger or zigzag stitch, finish the seam allowances together and press toward the back. Finish the bottom and back side edges of the facing.

17. Turn your dress so the right side is facing out. Pin the right side of the neck facing to the right side of the dress, raw edges together, with the facing's short ends aligned with the unsewn edges of the back panels, and with its seams aligned with the shoulder seams of the dress.

The facing will cover the top part of your zipper tape. Starting from the bottom of one short edge of the facing, sew toward the neckline using a ¼-inch seam allowance. Stop ¼ inch from the neckline, pivot, then sew the facing to the neckline, again using a ¼-inch seam allowance. Stop when you are ¼ inch from the seam allowance on the other side, and again pivot, sewing just to the bottom of the neck facing.

18. Press the seam allowance and the neck facing up and away from the dress. Starting 1 inch from the zipper, understitch the neckline by sewing the facing to the seam allowance very close to the seam. Stop understitching 1 inch from the neckline on the other side. Trim the seam allowance to just a little over ⅛ inch. Clip the seam allowance perpendicular to your stitches, careful not to cut your stitches. This will help the rounded areas to lie flat. Turn the facing to the inside of the neckline and press well. Pin the facing in place and press well, until the facing lies flat.

19. Beginning from one back panel, topstitch along the neckline ¼ inch from the edge.

20. Hem the dress: Fold the dress hem under ¼ inch toward the wrong side of the dress and press. Fold the hem under another 1 inch, and press again. Topstitch the hem by sewing close to the inside fold.

STEP
19

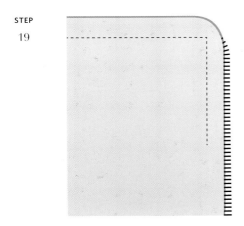

DESIGN IT YOURSELF!

- *SEW A SMALL PATCH POCKET OVER THE BUST AREA.*

- *MAKE THE SLEEVES FROM A CONTRASTING FABRIC.*

PATTERN CUTTING
INSTRUCTIONS

The pattern sheets for all of the projects in this book are included on the sheets attached to the back of this book. The sewing instructions in chapter 7 refer to the numbers on these pattern pieces, and each pattern piece is also clearly labeled.

Trace all of the pattern's pieces onto tracing paper or pattern paper, including all markings. You can then pin the traced pieces to your fabric or hold them in place with pattern weights while you cut out the pieces from your fabric.

TEMPLATES

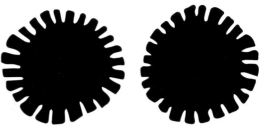

ANEMONE LEAF

CAMEO TULIP

CROCUS

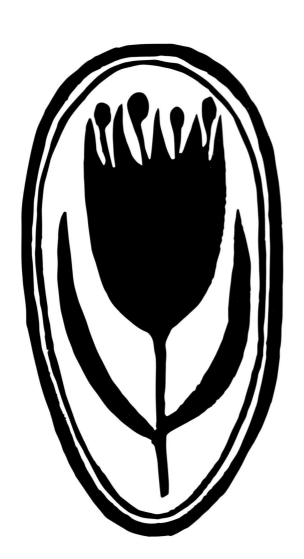

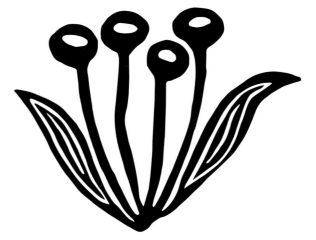

DOTS

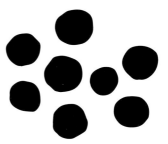

POPPY BORDER

OLIVE BRANCH

SCANDINAVIAN BLOOM

SCANDINAVIAN STEM

RESOURCES

FABRIC

The Fabric Store: The Fabric Store is my go-to fabric destination whenever I'm in Los Angeles. They have a huge selection of affordable, high-quality garment fabrics at www.thefabricstoreusa.com.

Robert Kaufman Fabrics: Robert Kaufman manufactures a wide range of garment fabric, including the Essex linen-cotton blends I have used extensively throughout this book. Available at fabric retailers worldwide and at www.robertkaufman.com.

ART SUPPLIES

Alvin and Company: Alvin manufactures my favorite utility knives and cutting mats. Available at art supply stores nationwide; you can find a retailer at www.alvinco.com.

Anthem Screen Printing: Anthem has a huge selection of screenprinting ink—and the friendliest shop animals. If you can't visit their store in South San Francisco, you can order online at www.anthem printingsf.com.

Dick Blick Art Materials: Blick has a huge selection of art supplies. If you can't find something in one of the stores, it's usually available online at www.dickblick.com.

BOOKS

Block Printing: Techniques for Linoleum and Wood by Robert Craig (Stackpole Books, 2011).

Block Printing on Textiles by Janet Erickson (Watson-Guptill, 1974).

The Complete Photo Guide to Clothing Construction by Christine Haynes (Creative Publishing International, Inc., 2014).

Fashionary Womens A5 sketchbook from Fashionary International Ltd. (fashionary.org).

How to Speak Fluent Sewing by Christine Haynes (Stash Books, 2015).

Teaching Fabric Printing in Schools: The Indispensable Illustrated Guide to Sewing and Fabric Terminology by H. Wooller (Evan Brothers Limited, 1937).

ACKNOWLEDGMENTS

Although the nuns in my elementary school would have said it's impossible to have four best friends, I consider myself lucky to have four BFFs in my life: Lisa Congdon, whose daily texts of snark, humor, and encouragement keep me going, and the three O.G.'s: Stephanie Dodaro, Yvonne Shen, and Stacy Tolchin, who have been my constant cheerleaders since the days we were all broke twenty-somethings who bought two-dollar bottles of wine.

To the Awesomes—Amelia Strader, Liz Kalloch, and Stef Lindeen—the best art-lady support group a working artist could ask for.

To Sonya Philip, who wasn't my first sewing teacher but who was the person who showed me how to sew well-finished garments, and who encouraged me to enjoy the process and forgive myself when I make mistakes.

To Nichole Ramirez of Robert Kaufman Fabrics, who so graciously provided much of the fabric I used in this book.

To Isobel Schofield, of Bryr Clogs, for contributing the gorgeous clogs I wear throughout the book. Bryr's shoes perfectly complement my garments, and Bryr's business ethic pairs so well with my own.

To Barrie Brouse and Kenny Liang, who developed such beautiful clothing patterns from my very rough sketches, creating something even more incredible than I'd expected. Every package I received from them was a joy to open.

To Marie Muscardini of the beautiful Handcraft Studio School, who has provided me with a teaching home and a wonderful community of students. I owe much of my development as a teacher to classes I've taught at HSS.

To my agent, Kate Woodrow, who so kindly popped out of her maternity leave to help me navigate the end bits of the proposal process.

To the hundreds of people who have taken my classes, and who have taught me as much about teaching and learning as I hope I've taught them about block printing.

And, finally, the hugest of thank-yous goes out to the other two Jen(n)s who were instrumental in the creation of this book: my photographer, Jen Siska, and my editor, Jenn Urban-Brown. Jen captured the vision I had for this book perfectly, and her photos are a reflection, not only of her immense talent, but also of the great working relationship we developed throughout the course of its development. From the moment she first contacted me about writing a book, Jenn understood exactly what I wanted to do, and pushed me to improve on my initial idea. I've heard that this kind of relationship is rare, and I feel so lucky to have had Jenn's encouragement and guidance all along.

ABOUT THE AUTHOR

Jen Hewett is a San Francisco–based printmaker, surface designer, and teacher. She and her dog, Gus, live in a beautiful, light- and art-filled apartment two blocks from Golden Gate Park and two miles from the Pacific Ocean. Since 2014, she has taught block printing to hundreds of students around the world through her popular in-person and online classes. In addition to designing and printing her own collections, Jen also creates custom, limited-edition products for retail clients. Visit her at www.jenhewett.com.